D1401477

GREENDALE

The Little Village
That Could...
and Did

The true story about Wisconsin's "Greenbelt Town",
told by people who live there.

Editor: Hal Prey
Copy Editor: Kristine Krueger
Art Director: Judy Larson
Art Assistant: Maribeth Greinke-Fleischmann
Photo Coordinator: Trudi Bellin
Illustrator: Jim Sibilski
Graphic Art Associates: Ellen Lloyd, Catherine Fletcher

@ 2004 Reiman Media Group, Inc.
5400 S. 60th St., Greendale WI 53129

Country Books
International Standard Book Number: 0-89821-411-4
Library of Congress Control Number: 2004093567
All rights reserved. Printed in U.S.A.

For additional copies of this book or information on other books,
write: Country Books, P.O. Box 990, Greendale WI 53129.
Credit card orders call toll-free 1-800/558-1013.

IMAGES OF GREENDALE

The following organizations and persons contributed the photographs that appear on these pages. The memorable moments they captured have added an indelible visual dimension to this history of the village. We are grateful to them.

Greendale Historical Society
Resettlement Administration
Library of Congress, Farm Security
   Administration Collection, John Vachon
Library of Congress, Prints & Photographs
   Division, FSA-OWI collection
Tri-Town News (Hales Corners)
Reiman Publications

G. Hickok
Ed Bengs
Alvin Basse
Carol Rosencrantz
Jack C. Murdaugh
John Kuglitsch
John Hermes

How Greendale Grew...

CONTENTS

This Book Had a Whole Lot of 'Editors'

WE ARE deeply indebted to a large group of people for their help in producing this "history of Greendale".

First and foremost, we thank the members of the Greendale Historical Society for their support and help in gathering the narrative background of our beloved community. They searched through scrapbooks, family albums, newspaper clippings and miscellaneous items, and also shared their memories.

We are especially grateful to Historical Society President Sally Chadwick for her ever-cheerful encouragement and hours of dedication—she provided names, dates and sources…then read this whole book *twice* and some parts three times to assure its accuracy.

We also thank Quentin Zillig, Ted Mainella, Bill Poglitsch, Carol Curtin, Jim Curtin, Roy Reiman, Dorothy Fischbach and Diana Munger for all the time they spent arranging and conducting interviews with the more than 70 residents who shared their experiences of life in early Greendale. Their personal recollections included in these pages provide an invaluable recounting of the human spirit as a new frontier of suburban living unfolded. The reminiscences of these pioneers—some of whom are no longer with us—add a fascinating personal dimension to this telling of a modern urban miracle.

No one, though, deserves more credit than this book's editor, Hal Prey, who spent a good part of 3 years gathering the facts, figures, photos and anecdotes compiled here. He, as well as we, thought we knew this village well…but we learned so much more to appreciate in the process.

Greendale really is a special town, with a unique history and a lot of really special people.

The Story of Greendale...from Vision to Reality

EVEN TODAY, it's exciting to hear or read of a new community that's being planned, one being built in a country venue that will include a shopping center, schools, parks and an abundance of new homes.

It's even more impressive when you learn that this kind of progressive planning happened *back in 1934*, when a group of visionaries in the Roosevelt Administration gathered to select sites to design and build three "Greenbelt Towns".

Over 100 major cities were first considered...the selection was then narrowed to eight...and finally Milwaukee was one of the three chosen. The latter selection was partly due to the large, attractive tract of rolling farmland on the city's southern border—it seemed a perfect fit for the designers' plan.

Just imagine that group's challenge back then, as they walked over this land—*3,410 acres* of it—and decided where to put the business center, the schools, the parks

and hundreds of homes, plus where to place the streets, etc. But accomplish it they did, creating one of the prettiest villages in all of the Midwest.

This town was named "Greendale". When it was finished, the challenge of its designers and builders was matched by the pioneers who moved here—572 families, each selected basically because they were poor. They would all be renters, albeit at a reasonable rate, and the U.S. government would be their landlord.

This book brings you the story of the builders and the settlers, much of it in their own words, illustrated with more than 250 photos, many from family albums. Their words and memories allow you to immerse yourself in the spirit of these pioneers, who made it possible for Greendale to grow from a novel idea to the charming, historical village it is today.

So find yourself a comfortable chair—once you begin, you're going to be reading awhile. Enjoy!

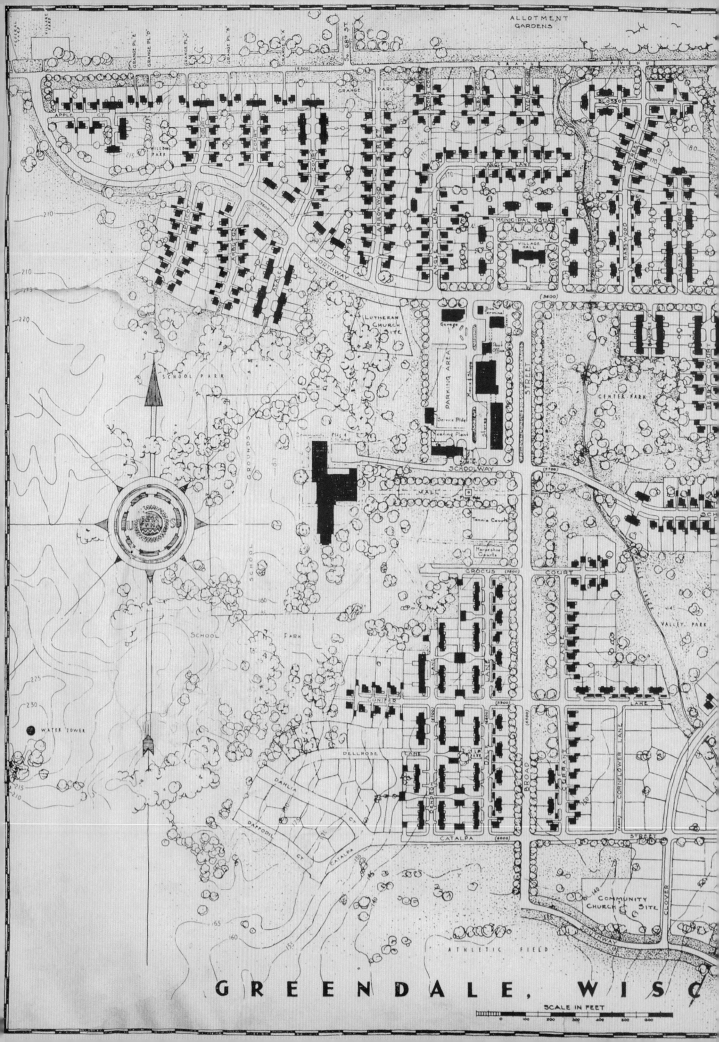

GREENDALE, WISC

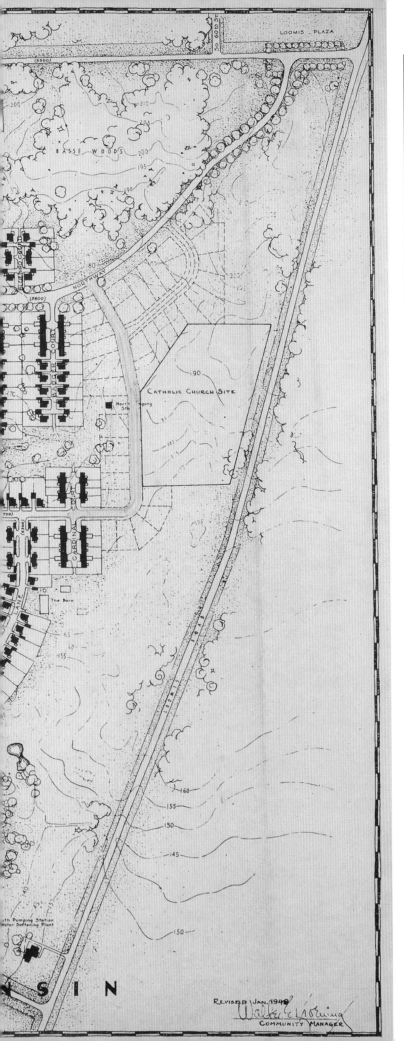

LOOMIS PLAZA

BASSE WOODS

NORTHWAY

CATHOLIC CHURCH SITE

CARDINAL COURT

LANE

The Barn

CARDINAL

Pumping Station
Water Softening Plant

S I N

REVISED JAN. 1948
COMMUNITY MANAGER

A Neighborly Way of Life

THIS MAP was prepared in 1934. It's the blueprint of Greendale as its planners envisioned turning more than 3,000 acres of farmland into a new type of urban community.

They decided to set the village's original homes amid a unique pattern of curving, "functional" thoroughfares to discourage undue traffic and ensure personal safety. They designed its main street—called Broad Street—to dead-end at the Village Hall, the heart of the community.

They formed borders around the village center with roads called "ways"—Northway, Eastway, Southway and Westway. The outer limits of the village were defined by Grange Avenue on the north, Loomis Road on the east, Root River Parkway on the south and 92nd Street on the west.

They designated narrower roads as "lanes", "courts" and "cul-de-sacs" to serve the homes. To make it easier for work crews to find locations during construction—and to serve new residents in the same way later—sections were "alphabetized".

The names of courts and lanes in one section begin with the letter A (Angle Lane, Apricot Court, e.g.), the second section's names all begin with B, the next section's with C, etc.

As the village expanded, this unique alphabetical identification has endured. When a resident says, "I live in the M section," another resident immediately knows where that is.

The designers even gave considerable thought to a distinctive network of paved pedestrian paths that wind behind and between the yards, providing every home a pleasant, traffic-free walk to playgrounds, schools and the village center. These paths were purposely made narrow to "encourage walkers to meet, chat and get acquainted".

The designers wanted Greendale to become a neighborly "community". They certainly succeeded.

CHAPTER 1

> "My wife said, 'We're going to move to Greendale.' My reaction was, 'Way out there in the sticks??' She said, 'Yes, out in the sticks. They've got nice homes, and I think we'd like it out there.' I said, 'Well, okay.'"
> —Clarence Klett

> "I remember thinking that all the houses looked alike. And it really looked barren to me because there were hardly any trees. But, after living for years in a furnished apartment, I quickly learned to enjoy the freedom and privacy."
> —Karen Erickson Fogelberg

> "Getting acquainted with all the new neighbors was very easy since everyone was a stranger to each other. We were all in the same circumstances, young people raising children and living on small incomes. Everyone got along well and was always ready to give a helping hand to anyone in trouble. It was a great experience."
> —Jim Kendellen

> "We liked the area. We thought it would be a nice place to live and bring up children. And it truly was."
> —Stanley and Marian Prey

> "The neighborhood was great. Everybody had about three or four children, and our street was like a wonderful playground for them."
> —Sigmund and Alice Tylenda

> "I always felt safe when our kids walked around the village. And we never locked our doors at night. I don't think anybody did." —Emma Hill

572 Families Took a Chance on Greendale

THEY HAD ALL COME to live in a village called "Greendale", lush with gentle hills, thick woods, nearby farms, interspersed with numerous lakes and ponds tucked invitingly around a 700-acre park.

They and 566 other families would be pioneers in a new concept in family living.

It was all so very new, so *different* from life in the city. No more crowded apartments, small yards and busy streets, and no more rejections by landlords because of children.

The United States Government was their landlord. All these homes were rented from the government, and children were welcome. But as the pioneer Greendale families soon discovered, even the new landlord had a rule about children.

"If you had two boys or two girls, you could have a two-bedroom home," recalls Roberta Henrichs. "But if you had a boy and a girl, you had to move into a three-bedroom home. That was the rule."

The new skyline emerging some 8 miles southwest of the city of Milwaukee was a unique response to a pair of crises engulfing the nation:

1. The stock market crash of 1929 and the resulting Great Depression had left millions of Americans unemployed and liv-

ing in crowded U.S. city slums. More than half of the houses in cities could not meet the criteria of a decent home.

2. In rural areas, unimaginable dust storms blew away the livelihood of farmers who took to the road in desperation and became the "Okies" of our nation's history, picking up work wherever they could find it.

The crises created a pressing need to create a new lifestyle and, at the same time, alleviate unemployment. The notion of new homes in new towns beyond the industrial centers of major cities intrigued political and social planners alike.

Similar communities dating back to the 1920s had been developed in a number of major metropolitan areas. But the "greenbelt design", modeled after early-1800s English garden homes, seemed like an idea whose time had come.

The "Greenbelt Towns" concept officially became a reality as part of President Franklin Delano Roosevelt's "New Deal" policy. On April 30, 1935, he signed an executive order authorizing the resettle-

ment of "destitute and low-income families from rural areas".

A special relief agency, the Resettlement Administration, was created to supervise the project. The concept was soon expanded to ease the plight of city dwellers, too. The policy move was also seen as an opportunity to solve the deepening unemployment crisis.

While the Greenbelt Towns de-

> ## "President Roosevelt signed the order, and 3,410 acres were bought for $1.2 million…"

sign was applauded, its birth was not easy. The overall concept became caught up in a tangle of conflicting political, economic and social visions, as well as plans of politicians, bureaucrats, environmental planners and local community leaders. Everybody, as one could expect, got into the act.

Early in the planning process, many referred to the suburban

THE WAY IT WAS. This was 51st Street, looking south, in 1934. This rural gravel road would see some big changes in the years immediately ahead.

Greenbelt Towns as "Tugwell Towns", confusing them with earlier rural communities. The moniker was derived from the name of Resettlement Administrator Rexford G. Tugwell, who was involved in the planning of both types of communities.

Finally, compromises were hammered out, involving planning and design, site selections, purchases of needed tracts of land—and, not the least, the politics of locating a bold, innovative community near an established one with the government as landlord.

More than 60 sites were considered at one point. Greendale, despite some anxious nail-biting, survived, along with Greenbelt, Maryland, near Washington, D.C.; and Greenhills, Ohio, near Cincinnati. A fourth site—Greenbrook near New Brunswick, New Jersey—made it to the final selection process, but political opposition forced the government to abandon its plans there.

Milwaukee owed its selection as the location of a Greenbelt Town to a variety of factors:

1. It had a multifaceted and steadily growing industrial base.

2. On the southwestern fringe of Milwaukee lay hundreds of acres of agricultural land that could be acquired.

3. Enthusiastic support for the Greenbelt Town project seemed assured in a city famed for its socialist politics.

4. The German-American character of the city, one report contended, was another point in its favor because Germanic people were known for their industriousness, their thrift and their love of horticulture, music, art and drama.

No Time to Waste

As it turned out, the Resettlement Administration (RA) encountered less opposition in Milwaukee than in any other city. This was likely due in part to the fact that RA officials met with Milwaukee Mayor Daniel Hoan early in the project to fully explain the program and enlist his support.

Once the decision for the Greendale site was reached, things had to move quickly, due to the rules set by the government. On April 8, 1935, Congress had enacted the Emergency Relief Appropriations Act,

providing over $4 billion (the largest single appropriation in American history) for public works projects that would provide work for the unemployed in the midst of the Depression.

Tugwell pitched his idea to President Roosevelt. A believer in the benefits of country living, the President responded enthusiastically.

On September 12, 1935, Roosevelt allocated $31 million to the RA for the Greenbelt Towns program, with the implication that an additional $38 million might be granted in the future.

Not only was the budget smaller than hoped for, it was further encumbered by the requirement that all the land for the towns had to be purchased by December 15, 1935, and that the towns must be completed by June 30, 1936!

Tugwell proposed expanding the Greenbelt approach to the construction of new towns outside large industrial cities across the nation, but he was turned down with sort of a "Let's walk before we run" advisement from Roosevelt.

Tugwell later stated: "My idea was to go just outside cities of population, pick up cheap land, build a whole new community and entice people to move there. Then go back into the cities and tear down whole

slums and make parks of them."

A panel of four men from the RA studied 100 major industrial cities to determine where to locate Greenbelt Towns. Twenty-five cities were determined to meet the criteria, and further consideration narrowed the list to eight: St. Louis, Cincinnati, Milwaukee, Chicago, New Brunswick, Dayton, Chattanooga and Washington, D.C.

Milwaukee, Cincinnati and Washington, D.C. were the eventual winners.

Land Purchase Begins

The option-to-buy process for the land was started in southwestern Milwaukee County by the RA in August 1935. Harold Gelnaw, a Washington-based real estate broker, was put in charge of optioning land.

Faced with resistant landowners and a deadline of November 20 for securing all the options, Gelnaw resorted to threats that he would have the land condemned and even planted a rumor that the land was needed for a munitions factory.

Agents negotiating the Greendale site on behalf of the U.S. Government did so quietly without reveal-

MEMBERS of the Resettlement Administration (often referred to as the RA) gathered for a party in 1936.

ing the full intent of the project so as not to drive up the price.

By December 1935, when actual purchasing began, Gelnaw had optioned 10,760 acres. Of this, the RA eventually bought 3,410 acres at a cost of $1.2 million. That made the average price per acre $372, about $100 more per acre than at Greenhills, Ohio and $200 more than at Greenbelt, Maryland.

Each Greenbelt Town project had its own design team. Greendale's staff was led by Elbert Peets (1886-1968), the chief planner, who was born in Hudson, Ohio and received his degree in landscape architecture from Harvard University in 1915.

Over 100 people were part of the Greendale team, including support personnel and consultants in diverse fields such as real estate analysis, agricultural practices and wildlife management.

The Greendale team was headquartered with other project teams in the Washington mansion of socialite Lady Evelyn Walsh McLean.

A local office for the Greendale project was soon opened in Madison. Field research for the project—including topographical surveys and social research on blue-collar families in Milwaukee—was also carried out from the Madison office.

Families Surveyed

While the designers labored to prepare the plans, several thousand questionnaires were distributed to members of Milwaukee labor unions, churches, civic groups and ethnic associations.

More than 2,000 surveys were returned, but only the 1,000 that came from families reporting annual incomes in the target "moderate" range—between $1,000 and $2,400 —were tabulated.

Families in the target income range spent, on average, $21 to $28 per month in rent, according to the surveys. It was decided rents in Greendale would match this spread.

In addition, the survey returns revealed community amenities that future Greendale residents hoped to

DALE CREEK was a narrow stream running through a farm pasture before Greendale construction began. This view looks south toward Schoolway.

enjoy: A flower garden (94%), vegetable garden (92%) and library (86%) were the most desired. A swimming pool (79%), community hall (61%) and baseball fields (57%) were popular choices, too.

Respondents also requested some amenities that weren't on the survey form, and several of them were accommodated, including a movie theatre, drugstore, barbershop, service station, health services, and village fire and police services.

Although 90% had requested a church of their denomination, constitutional law—even back then— prohibited the government from building churches. However, it was stated that church services could be held in the Community Building (and they were), and the plan did set aside several sites for future church construction.

CHAPTER 2

How Greendale Got Its Name

A LADY whose name deservedly belongs on Greendale's pioneer roster, Agnes Strong, was associated with the project even before the Milwaukee area was selected for a "Greenbelt Town" site. She had the honor of being its first local employee.

At the time, Agnes was employed by a Milwaukee real estate agent who had a contract with the federal government to secure options on the Greendale tract. She checked titles, platted legal descriptions and prepared maps.

After the government opened an office in Milwaukee, Agnes became secretary to the negotiator who was in charge of land acquisitions.

"My job involved checking land titles back to the early 1800s. Our work had to be thorough and painstaking," she recalled in an interview printed in 1940. "The government attorneys insisted on clear titles.

"We had some tough problems. In some cases, we had to visit cemeteries to get the required information.

"You know, Greendale didn't even have a name in those days," she added. "We simply called it 'The Project'."

Subsequently, Agnes became secretary to Fred Naumer, a Re-

ELBERT PEETS, a nationally known town planner, designed the initial layout of Greendale in 1936. His goal was to preserve as much natural beauty as possible while creating a community for practical living. He also served as a consultant when the expansion was planned in the 1940s.

settlement Administration regional coordinator in charge of the project. And when Greendale became a reality, she was named secretary to Community Manager Sherwood Reeder.

With its selection, Greendale lost the "Tugwell Town" label some had given it, and, on March 24, 1936, was officially christened "Greendale" by Tugwell and J.S. Lansill, director of the suburban division of the RA.

Greendale's name is attributed to Fred Naumer. He noted the name was symbolic of the three Greenbelt communities and that "dale" was particularly descriptive of the area's gently rolling hills and ponds. The name simply "fit".

Of the 3,410 acres purchased for the Greendale site, 2,800 acres were farmland. The rest was undeveloped wooded land.

There were 14 dairy farms, ranging from 75 to 240 acres...one large poultry farm housing some 1,200 hens ...a truck farm of 50 acres... one cattle feeding farm...plus 49 small farms of 1 to 10 acres each and a riding academy. One large farm, comprising 235 acres, was operated by Francis Moss.

William and Rose Basse owned another large farm, located on the south side of Grange Avenue, stretching from about 63rd Street west to 76th Street.

"My parents received $350 an acre from the government for it," recalls Ruth (Basse) Klussendorf, now living in North Aurora, Illinois. "Our farmhouse became a teacher's dormitory and later was the first clubhouse of the Greendale American Legion. My two brothers, Robert and Alvin, and I were born in that house."

Some of these farms had been leased by the government to private individuals, who were sometimes referred to as "Greendale Ruralites". Most of the smaller farms were operated on a part-time basis, with the head of the family holding down another job.

The leased farms were under the supervision of Max Sievers, who assisted the tenants as an advisor on farming problems.

The Greendale site was designed by Elbert Peets, a nationally acclaimed town planner. He was assisted by Jacob Crane, a city planning consultant. The Greendale homes were designed by Harry Howe Bentley, while Walter G. Thomas planned its public buildings. The other two members of the project team were Fred Naumer and Charlton Putnam.

Peets also collaborated in two other Wisconsin projects—the village of Kohler, near Sheboygan; and Washington Highlands in Wauwatosa, a suburb west of Milwaukee.

> ## "The workforce peaked at 2,000 in October of 1936…"

Originally, 750 living units were planned for Greendale, with 23 different types of house plans. That was eventually trimmed back to 366 buildings with 572 dwelling units.

Of the 366 buildings constructed, there were 274 single-family houses, 45 two-unit "twins", 10 three-unit row houses, 22 four-unit row houses and 15 six-unit row houses. Of the 274 single-family structures, 230 had three bedrooms and 44 had two bedrooms.

Nearly all were two-story homes, except for a few one-bedroom units. Only childless couples were eligible for the one-bedroom units, and as a result, these small homes were nicknamed "Honeymooners".

The arrangement of many of the single-house dwellings was highly unusual. Called "chain house" siting, each house is offset on its lot, built close to the street and along the sideline of the lot, creating an L-shaped yard.

The garage is attached to the rear corner of the neighboring house, linking the houses and garages along each side of the street like a chain, and forming a court between each pair of houses.

Peets referred to the court as a "Hof", a term used in Germany to refer to the space around which the buildings in European farm villages were arranged.

Workers Paid $2 an Hour

The Works Progress Administration (WPA) was put in charge of construction and began hiring unemployed workers who were on relief. Skilled workers were paid as much as $2 an hour while unskilled laborers received 50¢ an hour.

Thousands of men desperate for work poured into the area. During the early stages of the construction, as many as 250 additional men were hired each day.

The first shovel of the soil that was to nurture Greendale was turned over in April 1936, with a crew of 332 men. Greendale's workforce would peak at about 2,000 in October of 1936. Those seeking work and a new way of life faced an exciting future.

The workers' first task was to build a 3-mile-long railroad spur connecting to an electric rail line so they could haul equipment to the construction site.

Tracks for the spur were laid through the area on which Southridge Shopping Center was later

BASSE FARM south of Grange Avenue was one of the farms bought by the government to develop Greendale.

CONSTRUCTION BEGINS. First shovel of dirt was moved in April 1936. Photo above was taken near South 76th Street where Southridge Shopping Center is now located.

3-MILE RAILROAD SPUR (below) was one of the first things built to facilitate hauling equipment to the construction site. These tracks were laid north of Grange near 76th Street.

built. That area served as a storage depot for construction materials. (The berm for that spur is still visible west of 76th Street on the Martin Luther High School grounds.)

Unfortunately, early construction was hampered by weather extremes. Temperatures topped 100 degrees in the summer and dropped to below zero in the winter. Adding to the daily work discomfort in spring were heavy rains, creating a sea of mud.

Most of the laborers were paid through the WPA, which also provided them with rudimentary equipment such as picks, shovels and horse-drawn wagons.

As summer moved into fall, the project lagged far behind schedule while the man-hours expended mounted alarmingly. A frustrated Tugwell reportedly told President Roosevelt the laborers must have been issued *spoons*, at the pace the work was going.

The work was extremely labor-intensive, slowed by the deliberate use of horse-drawn road graders, wagons and hand shovels. The decision delayed completion schedules, but it had the benefit of guaranteed added jobs. An average of 1,600 men were employed during the 2-year start-up construction.

Budget Problems Surface

By October 15, Greendale's planners realized that costs would far exceed the $7 million budget, and they reluctantly decided to defer the construction of all housing not already under way. The infrastructure had been built first, so all the streets, water and sewer lines needed for the town of 1,200 families were already in place.

To stay within budget, the design team made the decision to cut back from the 750 living units originally planned and finish the 572 units already started. The additional farmland being readied was then repaired and leased out.

Budgetary problems also surfaced in the other two Greenbelt Towns.

MORE GRADING was needed as the rail spur continued west toward 84th Street. Lots of horsepower was used.

Due to cost overruns, the Greenbelt, Maryland project was reduced to 885 dwelling units, and the Greenhills, Ohio project to 676 units.

However, this meant the federal government would have to retain ownership of all three towns for the foreseeable future. The towns could not be turned over to a local co-operative housing authority because they would have too few residents and businesses to generate sufficient rents to support necessary municipal services and amortize the debt.

On the other hand, retaining ownership of the towns had the benefit of protecting the communities' undeveloped land from unscrupulous developers. This also allowed the government the opportunity to complete the communities as originally intended, should the funds become available in the future.

CHAPTER 3

Early Resident's
'Before and After'
Thoughts

AN ANONYMOUS CONTRIBUTOR writing in the October 20, 1938 issue of *The Greendale Review*—a mimeographed, letter-size bulletin that served as the village's first newspaper—voiced his/her feelings about the advantages of leaving crowded substandard urban housing for a new way of life in a place called "Greendale":

Before we moved to Greendale…

John, the landlord, had raised the rent. "Don't worry, dear, we'll find something…" "Children? No thanks, adults only…" "You can't afford that much? Sorry, but we feel we'll get it if we hold out with the housing shortage. We had twenty couples look at it yesterday…"

"Nothing doing on a lease, we can't guarantee not to raise the rent, rents may go even higher…" "Thirty-five dollars for that shack? No bath, stove heat, toilet in the basement…" "Don't give up, Daddy, maybe the Sunday classifieds will have just the place…"

"Keep your chin up, Mom. Surely, somewhere there must be a landlord with a heart, who won't object to children…" "There must be a decent place with rent we can afford to pay…"

"Why, of course, there is. Greendale…Applied…Accepted!"

After we moved to Greendale…

One-year lease…brand-new house…fireproof. No living in mortal fear that the old shack would go up in flames and the family with it…real honest-to-goodness plumbing.

No sharing the bath with strangers living in the apartment house…utility room on the first floor…no stumbling up and down cellar stairs…thousands of steps saved for mother…a real dream kitchen…light…air…cleanliness… electric refrigeration…electric range.

No food to spoil because the iceman missed us over the weekend…no odors of gas and no cooking heat in hot weather…beamed ceiling in living room…cross ventilation in bedrooms.

On the outside…a yard, brother, a real yard! Kids playing…flowers…lawn…shrubs. And the air…boy, oh, boy, it's different…clean, clear, fresh, no soot, no smoke, no odors.

A first-class heating unit…insulation…no $100 coal bill this winter…just half of that, and we'll all be as snug as so many bugs in a rug!

HOUSE CONSTRUCTION began in 1936. View above looks north toward Grange Avenue. Originally, 750 living units were planned, but budget cuts reduced it to 572.

MINIATURE MODEL (below) gave prospective tenants an idea of what the new homes would look like. Note closeness of house to the street to maximize size of backyard.

'The Project Is Attracting a Lot of Attention'

THIS LARGE INNOVATIVE housing project hardly went unnoticed. More than 80% of those who applied for a Greendale home said they had heard about it through the local newspapers.

One of the first homes completed, on 5503 Acorn Street, was opened as a model in February 1937. As the village took shape, more people came to satisfy their curiosity.

Hundreds of visitors toured this model home on weekends, and it remained a popular attraction until it was rented to Mr. and Mrs. Harry Nelezen and their family on March 1, 1939. Later that year, a second model home was opened at 5812 Currant Lane.

Spending Sunday afternoons driving up and down the streets of Greendale became a favorite pastime for thousands of curious Milwaukeeans as well as visitors from more distant places.

Even before the homes were ready for occupancy, more than a *half million people* visited Greendale between September 1936 and August 1937, it was reported.

"We've had more company in the last 3 months than we had in the first 15 years of our married life!" said one Greendale housewife, according to *The Milwaukee Journal*.

Among the visitors were Dora Crowley Ariens and her fiance, Monroe. "We followed the progress of this wonderful program for people of our income level," she recalls.

A Dream Come True

"Those were the Depression years, and *The Milwaukee Journal* was full of exciting news when this area was chosen as one of the sites for a Greenbelt Town…and the work would be done with WPA labor to create jobs for the unemployed. This was a dream!

"Monroe and I became engaged in 1936 and were married the following year," Dora continues.

"All through those months, we'd drive out on Sunday afternoons in Monroe's 1931 Model A Ford Roadster to marvel at the gradual changing of farmland into homes and streets. We were thrilled at each stage of progress."

Early photos show traffic jams on Grange Avenue on Sunday afternoons. Another draw to the area were the farms surrounding Greendale. Several of the new houses had barns in their backyards.

"The Van Alstine farm had cows and a big apple orchard where you could pick bushes of apples," remembers Viola Eilers. "There were nut trees, too. It was just wild land the government owned, and you could pick whatever you wanted."

"My husband, Arnold, walked the dog about a half mile to the Van Alstine farm every morning for a gallon of milk," Eileen Campbell recalls. "Often, I let it sit out, then took the cream off the milk and made ice cream with it."

John Miller well remembers the Van Alstine farm, too. "We took our 2-gallon milk can to Van Alstine, and he would pull his large milk cans out of the cold water and fill ours," John says. "I remember the milk was 25¢ a gallon."

TRAFFIC JAMS were common on Grange Avenue on Sunday afternoons as curious Milwaukeeans came for a look at the "Greendale project". On a special "Guest Day", Oct. 9, 1938, over 4,000 people showed up! Note construction shacks south of Grange in background.

ASSEMBLY-LINE FASHION was used throughout construction. Above, multiple foundations were laid.

HOME BELOW was finished early and used as "walk-through model". Thousands came for an up-close look.

CHAPTER 4

Who Would Be Lucky to Live There?

CHOOSING RESIDENTS to live in Greendale was the responsibility of the Resettlement Administration. Eligibility hinged on a family's income and number of children.

Since part of the project's aim was to help low-income families, the allowable annual income range was $1,000 to $2,400, with only larger families eligible at the higher end.

It's worth noting that only the husband's income was considered. If a wife held a job, her earnings were not counted because it was assumed she would soon quit work and start a family. In fact, the former was a requirement.

Evelyn Truppe was ready to give up her job, as the government required, when she and her husband, Walter, were both employed at Allen-Bradley. They moved to a small unit on Azalea Court in April of 1939.

"Wally called me from work and asked, 'Did you quit your job today?' I said, 'No, I decided to do it at the end of the week.'

"He told me, 'Don't. Allen-Bradley just went out on strike. I don't have a job right now.'

"Well, the strike lasted 5 months, and we had to live on my salary, which was $19 a week. Our rent was $19 a month, so things were tight.

"We didn't go anywhere very much during those months. I can remember one day when friends were coming to visit us, I said to Wally, 'I hate this. I can't even go out and buy anything to treat them with.'

"Wally replied, 'Give 'em lemonade. They're friends of ours. They'll understand.'

"It was rough going for a while. When Wally went back to work, I had to quit my job. The government watched that very closely."

Among the first to apply a year before the official opening were Dora and Monroe Ariens. They

"HONEYMOON HOUSE" was label residents gave the few smaller single-bedroom, one-story homes (right).

were accepted even though his salary of $65 a month as a drafting apprentice was considered too low. "The government allowed for the fact that he would be earning $150 a month when his apprenticeship ended," Dora explains.

"I was making $30 a week as a teller at a credit union, but my earnings were not counted. As it was, I would be quitting anyway because I became pregnant during our wait for the magical letter telling us when we could come to Greendale."

Almost another year passed before the Ariens received that eagerly awaited letter notifying them they could move into a two-bedroom unit on Dendron Lane in May.

"The very same day, Monroe came home from work with the news that his job was being cut down to 3 days a week," recalls Dora. "That meant only $48 a month. And with me expecting the baby in August, we decided to put off our move until then. That's also when

Monroe would go on full salary.

"The fee for delivering our baby girl, by the way, was $35, and my 10-day stay at the hospital cost $60,"

> ### *"Greendale was for those who earned $1,000 to $2,400 a year..."*

Dora adds. "To help pay the bills, we sold our Ford Roadster."

Sigmund and Alice Tylenda were told they didn't make enough money to qualify.

"So we applied at another housing project in the city, but there they told us we were making too much," recalls Sigmund. "So I went right back to them and asked what was going on.

"Well, when they saw the conditions we were living in, they backed off and told us they had a place for us on Azalea Court. We loved it

then, and we love it now. I hope it never changes."

On the other hand, Al and Eleanor Jolly were turned down that first year because their annual income was just $100 too high.

"Al had received a $100 bonus at work," Eleanor recounts, "and that put us over the acceptable level—we were making too much money for a couple with one child.

"That was the only year he'd ever gotten a bonus. The following year he didn't get one, and we became eligible to move into a two-bedroom unit in a two-family building on Azalea Court at the corner with Northway.

"After we had our second child, we were allowed to apply for a single home with three bedrooms," Eleanor adds.

STURDY TRESTLE was built west of 76th Street as 3-mile-long rail spur that continued west to connect to the rail line near Hales Corners.

Art and Leona Krueger, too, were over the salary limit, but by even less. "I was making $1,890 a year," Art remembers. "We were told that was $10 too much for a couple. "Then, Leona found out she was pregnant, so we reapplied and became eligible for a unit.

"We looked at a two-bedroom unit on Carnation Court. It was furnished with a refrigerator and electric stove, neither of which we had. We liked the beige color of the walls and the beams on the ceiling," Art says.

"We agreed, 'This is it, we're going to live here.' So we moved in with our bedroom set, two sofas, one of which could be turned into

a bed, plus a card table and apple crates that we used for chairs. Our rent was $27.50 a month."

Garage Was Extra

Rents ranged from $19 per month for a one-bedroom unit in a multi-family building to $32.50 per month for a four-bedroom single-family unit, with the average at $27.95. Rental of a garage cost an additional $2.50 a month.

Each unit included an electric stove...an electric refrigerator...a wall-mounted porcelain sink...metal kitchen cabinets...a bathroom that included a sink, tub and toilet...a forced-air furnace (coal fired), a laundry stove (coal fired), a coal storage closet and a concrete

THIS 1937 PHOTO has long been one of the favorites among those studying Greendale's history. Village Hall (circled) is yet to be built as assembly-line construction continues on houses between Northway and Grange Avenue.

laundry sink in the utility room.

Originally, Greendale's planners intended to furnish all the dwellings with furniture designed by the Resettlement Administration's Special Skills Division. But it had to be eliminated due to lack of funds.

That was perhaps for the best, since the young tenants likely preferred their own taste in furnishings. A high percentage of Greendale's pioneer tenants were between 25 and 34 years old.

LIVING UNITS were mostly single-family structures but included a few four-family row houses like one above (back side view below). The two gabled portions each had a small "bachelor apartment" above the garages.

CHAPTER 5

Houses Were Built 'Backward'

THE NEW HOUSES were constructed of cinder block and coated with a cement paint—in a bone white, yellow, green, gray, pink or cream color—which supposedly provided insulation. All the roofs had either red tile or gray shingles.

Each house was built close to the curb, as close as 20 feet, and positioned "backward". That is, the rear entrance of each home faced the street, and the large living room window faced the backyard.

Greendale's principal architect did this purposely because he reasoned most of these people had never had a lawn or garden before, and he wanted to maximize the backyard. Some of these spacious backyards were as large as 5,000 square feet. The architect described this as "gracious functionalism".

Nevertheless, this unusual design became the stuff of jokes. Critics, notably Milwaukeeans and their daily newspaper, *The Milwaukee Journal*, tossed such

barbs as "You people are guinea pigs"; "How can you stand those backward houses?" and "How can you find your house? They all look alike."

The exterior colors of Greendale's homes were what could be mildly termed a "riot of hues", featuring such shades as carnation pink, canary yellow, pea green and battleship gray.

The foresight of the designers in respect to small but important things is still appreciated today. Current residents often comment on how the designers obviously

CINDER BLOCK was used in all homes, then covered with cement paint. All had red or gray roofs.

'Imbibers' Stumbled into Wrong House

BRAMBLE BURKE, who lived on Municipal Square, was once awakened around 2 o'clock in the morning by someone coming up the stairs. It turned out to be a neighbor living in a house that exactly duplicated Bramble's.

The hapless "intruder" didn't realize his mistake until he went into the bathroom and noticed the towels looked different. Bramble and the neighbor quickly straightened out the matter.

Early residents smilingly report the same thing sometimes happened when the proprietor of the town tavern hosted "Whistle Hour". There weren't "Happy Hours" then, so when business was slow, the owner would step outside and blow a loud whistle. Residents—primarily men—would then know they could get "two for one" for the next hour.

Well, remember, most of the houses in the project looked exactly alike, especially at night when the exterior color wasn't obvious…and especially for those who had been imbibing.

Remember, too, no one locked their doors back then. Some of the pioneers still chuckle at the results.

---

had a great awareness of the setting of each house in reference to the sun.

"I always notice and appreciate how much sunlight we get in our home," an owner of an "original" said recently, "and how few windows there are on the north side of the house."

As for Greendale's roads, they were also designed to be "functional". Roads that lead through the village and connect with main highways are called "streets". Its "main drag", Broad Street, dead-ends at the Village Hall.

Other main roads within the village are called "ways"—the village center is bordered by Northway, Westway, Southway and Eastway. These thoroughfares provide convenient "compass points" for the lost motorist.

All main thoroughfares taper into narrower roads called "lanes" and "courts" or "cul-de-sacs". The three blocks completing the square around the Village Hall are appropriately named "Municipal Square".

A particularly distinctive feature of the original section of Greendale is its paved pedestrian paths, which

LOOK-ALIKES. This 1937 view looks north on Arrowwood Drive. It was sometimes hard to tell one home from another (see item at top of page).

Grange

Northway

were uniquely designed to run behind and between the yards, providing every home a pleasant, traffic-free walk to playgrounds, schools and the village center.

Early residents were told the architect purposely made these paths narrow; he felt that if people were forced to step to the side as they met, it would encourage greetings, conversation and a friendly sense of "community".

The streets and paths were designed so parents could walk safely to the post office, Community Building and stores, and so their children could play safely in their neighborhoods.

The easy walking distances fostered a closeness among the early families as they moved into this isolated community. Still today, residents say the best way to really see and enjoy Greendale is to bike or walk along these paths.

Despite the emphasis on design-

ing for safety, there's always the temptation to speed. The driver with the dubious distinction of being the first culprit arrested for speeding in

MAKING PROGRESS. Cinder blocks and roofs are in place and ready for the next work crew—hundreds of painters.

> *"The architect placed the living room window at the back for a better view of the yard…"*

the village shall remain unnamed here. But it can be reported that he paid a fine of $9.43 for driving down Broad Street at 46 miles per hour.

Some of Greendale's streets had temporary names during construction to make it easier to move workers and materials around the village.

But when it came to something more permanent, the village's unique traffic designs made naming the streets a dilemma. How would people ever find their way

around without some "system" they could relate to?

Walter Kroening, the chief design engineer for Greendale at the time, is credited with the village's unique street alphabetizing and section identification. All courts and lanes in one section were given names beginning with the letter A, the second section would have courts and lanes beginning with B, the next section with C and so on.

As he later recalled, "This became a family project for my family and our friends the Reeders. (Sherwood Reeder was appointed the first community manager by the Resettlement Administration.)

"The ladies did most of the work, digging out suitable garden city names from dictionaries in three languages. Postal authorities did not

permit duplication of names then being used in Milwaukee County.

"Finally, after several nights of preparation, we compiled a list as long as your arm of all possible names not yet used. It was evident that many—while of a fauna or floral nature—were not suitable.

"For instance, who would admit that his lawn was located on Dandelion Court or would want to live on Filbert Street?"

The Milwaukee Journal did a feature on this naming process and quoted a resident saying, "Everybody would think I'm a nut if I lived on Filbert Street!"

The idea worked perfectly. Greendalers simply say, "I live in the A section" (or the B, C or D section), and any other Greendaler immediately knows what section of town is being talked about.

The lanes and courts of the A section, which lies west of Dale Creek, are identified by colorful names like Acorn, Angle, Apple, Apricot, Arbutus, Azalea, Alba and Avena.

TWO-FAMILY HOUSE on Apple Court has a "bachelor apartment" above the garages in middle. Street sign at left—Azalea Court—is in the A section.

Courts and lanes in the B section, which is east of the creek, carry names such as Blossom, Balsam, Basswood, Berry, Bluebird, Beaver Bramble, Badger and Butternut.

The C section, in the southeast part of the village, contains signs reading Cornflower, Canterbury, Carnation, Conifer, Cardinal, Clover and Crocus. And in the D section, you'll find lanes and courts named Dendron, Daffodil, etc.

How names for the E section were selected is even more interesting. Sherwood Reeder, the first Village Manager, and Walter Kroening, Assistant Manager, sat around a kitchen table and pored over a map of London, copying down all street names that started with E!

As the village grew, subsequent sections have continued the alphabetical street designations.

CHAPTER 6

Almost All the Streets 'Bend'

THE BEAUTY of Elbert Peets' plan for Greendale was eloquently affirmed by Walter Wyrick, staff writer for *The Milwaukee Journal*, who wrote:

"Interestingly, Greendale's streets follow natural contours instead of running due north and south, and due east and west.

"Why cut down a beautiful tree? Why not wind the street around it or set the house back?

"Why have noisy, dusty traffic arteries in front of houses, making more work for the housewife and a deadly peril for young children?

Why not have the houses back on little service lanes, where there is freedom from traffic noises and where only private automobiles and occasional delivery trucks or the milk wagon travel? This is Greendale's plan."

Momentous Moving Day

As the project neared completion, the Resettlement Administration's Family Selection Section, which had been screening families for more than a year, stepped up its pace. It qualified more than 2,000 families in the 3-month period preceding the mo-

mentous "moving day".

The honor of becoming the first family to have its application approved for a dwelling in Greendale went to Mr. and Mrs. Allen Kroschin.

On May 1, 1938, almost 2 years to the day after building began, Greendale was officially ready to house families. Ten families were scheduled to occupy their new homes on that first day

CURVED STREETS were designed to follow natural contours of area. View is from west end of Northway.

PLANNING ROOM DEPARTMENT staffers had a big hand in Greendale's eventual appearance. Their office was in one of the construction sheds on south side of Grange Avenue.

WORKERS paused for picture (below). Jacob Adamick (fifth from left, back row) drove a team of horses during the construction, says his niece, Carol Rosencrantz.

of May, including the Kroschins and their two daughters, as well as Mr. and Mrs. Ernest Knutson and their four children, three boys and a girl.

A movers' strike hampered some of the residents' plans, but the new tenants were so eager to get into their new homes that it didn't stymie all of them.

"We didn't have that much furniture and belongings anyway, so we just rented a trailer and did the job ourselves," said Ernest Knutson, who with his wife and family were the very first people to arrive.

Even more eager than most to get into their new home on Apricot Court, Ernest loaded up the night before at his 70-year-old south side cottage and set out for Greendale very early the next morning—about 3 o'clock in the morning, in fact.

"I found the house locked," he told a *Milwaukee Journal* reporter. "There was nothing to do but unload the furniture on the driveway and drive back for another load. If it had been a rainy night, it would have been too bad, but the weather turned out perfect."

Fortunately, theft was not a problem in those days, and the untended furniture wasn't touched.

Finally, at 8:30 a.m., Ernest got a key from the Greendale project office. And after he got in, he enjoyed the first amenity of his family's new home—a bath. "We didn't have a bathtub in our old house," he explained.

Jim Kendellen, like so many of the other early dwellers, couldn't wait to make the move. "Our house on Arbutus Court had a garage, and

---

"The Resettlement Administration qualified more than 2,000 families in just 3 months..."

---

we didn't have a car, so we brought some things out here early and stored them in there.

"We were pleased with the refrigerator, electric stove, window shades and a hot water tank, and to learn that the coal bin in every home held a ton of coal," Jim said. "It was just a great pleasure to move into a new, clean home with brand-new appliances."

"That Hodgepodge"

One hundred families moved to Greendale during that first month, and one of the first to move into the B section was Chet Moehrlin's. He recalls being called into his boss' office in downtown Milwaukee.

"I walked in, wondering what I'd done wrong because it seemed that's the only time someone was called into his office," Chet says. "The boss greeted me, saying, 'Oh, you're the fellow who's going to move into that hodgepodge down there.'

"I replied, 'If you mean Greendale, that's right.'

"Then he said, 'Why do you want to move way out there?'

"I told him, 'With the salary I'm making, I feel I can qualify for one of the new houses, and we'd like to give it a try.'

"'Well, the RA people asked me if your job is secure and everything. It's all okay. Good-bye.'

"With that, he dismissed me. My wife and I applied for a home and were elated to be accepted. When we moved into one on Blossom Court, we were the 81st family to move into the village."

Among their neighbors were Mr. and Mrs. Carl Klein. When the Kleins became parents on July 2, 1938, theirs was the first baby born in a Greendale home.

SAND was loaded from a nearby sandpit in March 1936. It was used in making concrete foundations for houses.

LOTS OF HAND LABOR went into building Greendale. These men are digging a trench for a sewer along Apple Court.

CHAPTER 7

Look—Electric Stoves!

A BLEAK PICTURE was painted by a feature in *The Milwaukee Journal* right after the early arrivals moved in. Even when the movers' strike is over, it stated, the new residents would be facing challenges:

"The new tenants will find no grocery, no movie, no tavern and no department store. These services won't be established until late summer or fall.

"Meanwhile," the story went on, "the pioneers must travel to Hales Corners, 2 miles distant, or the outskirts of Milwaukee, 3 miles away, for their goods, dry or liquid."

At least one resident, Mrs. Joseph Switalski, told the reporter she didn't miss the corner grocery store. "The village is almost overrun with salesmen, trucks and farmers selling produce," she said.

Another challenge involved electricity. Greendale was one of the first towns in the country to

EVERY KITCHEN was furnished with an electric range and refrigerator.

TYPICAL LIVING ROOM of Greendale homes is shown above. Below is the infamous potbellied "monkey stove".

have its electrical and telephone lines installed underground. It eliminated telephone and light poles, but it was experimental.

Despite the shortcomings of the electrical system, early residents were pleased to have an electric stove, which was a novelty for those who'd previously used coal stoves.

Eileen Campbell particularly remembers the small potbellied coal stove—a "monkey stove", she called it—which she used to heat water for bathing and washing clothes.

Coal Was Still "King"

Emma Hill, too, remembers "that real monkey stove" in her new home. And Viola Eilers recalls, "We used to fire it up the night before and keep it burning to get enough hot water the next day; not just to wash our clothes, but to also dry them. We didn't have dryers then."

Even with the electric stoves, the homes still had coal bins for these small "heating" stoves.

"When the electricity went out, we couldn't use our regular stove since everything was electric," says Evelyn Truppe. "Even the furnace didn't work. So we'd have to start a coal fire in that little monkey stove and cook on it. We cooked many a meal of beans and wieners on it."

Evelyn loved her monkey stove and hated to give it up. "Later, when we got a new furnace, I used it as a planter in the garden."

Carol Curtin's mother had bought the family's first refrigerator just before they moved to Greendale and was a bit dismayed to learn one came with the new house. "She preferred her own refrigerator," says Carol. "She was allowed to keep it, and they took 50¢ off our electric bill each month for using our own refrigerator instead of one of theirs."

Regulation of the electric power was a source of irritation for residents at times.

Electric power for the village was purchased from the Wisconsin Electric Company, then resold to residents at a flat rate based on the appliances in use, including the stove and refrigerator.

Management (the government)

raised the issue of excessive individual electrical use on more than one occasion. Residents were sternly reminded not to use certain appliances that caused their electric power usage to exceed the limit set under their rental leases.

Unless the excessive use was curbed, they were told, electric rates would have to be increased.

Using the kitchen electric range to heat the kitchen was cited as the main "abuse". Other "no-no's" were using the electric range to heat water for laundry…burning lights unnecessarily…plugging in portable electric heaters in the winter…and turning on furnace blowers for cooling in the summer.

To solve the latter problem, servicemen were sent to the homes to install a device that prevented the blowers from running except when the furnace was turned on. Putting it mildly, some residents reacted belligerently, even preventing the workers from entering.

Sorry, No Humidifiers

Furthermore, residents were informed that electric vaporizers and humidifiers—despite being sold throughout the village—were not officially permitted.

Community Manager Sherwood Reeder felt it necessary to remind residents that "Proper humidity levels in the home can be maintained by keeping the water pan of the furnace filled at all times."

The matter was finally resolved, to some extent, by dividing the community into 20 areas, consisting of one or two streets, and each having its own meter.

If tenants in an area used more electricity than the area's allowance, they shared the additional cost equally. On the other hand, if they used less electricity than the area was allowed, their monthly charges were lowered proportionately. This policy effectively had the residents policing themselves.

KITCHENS were compact, as apparent in this '51 photo of Esther Woeste and her dog at 5607 Apricot Court.

THEY ALL HAD A HAND IN GREENDALE. This is the Re-settlement Administration staff, posing in front of their offices in Washington, D.C. The photo was taken Aug. 27, 1936.

TAKING SHAPE. Below is a photo taken on the hill at the west end of Northway, looking east as construction of this section of the village came closer to completion.

CHAPTER 8

Predictably, Eleanor Spoke Her Mind

THE INITIAL HOUSE PLANS had the coal bin sharing space with the laundry tubs in the first-floor utility room (there were no basements in the original Greendale homes). That meant each time coal would be shoveled down a chute into the room, coal dust settled over everything!

First Lady Eleanor Roosevelt came to the rescue. She took a personal tour of Greendale as part of a fast 36-hour stop in Milwaukee. As she toured the village and climbed up a ladder into one of its novel houses, she voiced a woman's view about coal bins and laundry tubs sharing the same room.

"Humph! You can tell a man designed this. A man should always have a woman at his elbow when he's planning these things," she reportedly remarked.

The reason that had been given by the architect, Harry Bentley, would not sit well with today's

THAT'S ELEANOR ROOSEVELT emerging from the door of one of the homes she toured on Nov. 11, 1936. She even climbed a ladder for a better view—and voiced her opinions.

37

CEMENT FLOORING was being poured for houses on Arbutus Court when this photo was taken Aug. 19, 1936.

housewife. "We combined the furnace and coal bin in the utility room with the laundry because the housewife has to do most of the coal shoveling, and it is more convenient to have it handy," he was quoted by *The Milwaukee Journal* in the summer of 1936.

"This way she can conveniently tend the furnace, do the washing, keep an eye on the cooking and watch the children."

Early resident Irene Kollross remembers Eleanor's reaction when she saw there wasn't a door on the coal bin.

"She said, 'The first thing you do is get doors on the coal bin. You are not having children play in the coal and run through the house and living room and get everything dirty. I am a mother. I know what can happen.'"

Mrs. Roosevelt's negative reaction had the desired effect. In no time at all, the coal bin and laundry tubs were separated by a door.

Despite these shortcomings, the First Lady remarked that Greendale was "absolutely wonderful and laid out beautifully," according to one news report.

Whether basements were ever a part of the plans for Greendale's homes has been bandied about over the years. Some of the village's pioneers still insist that Greendale was scheduled to have basements, but that its building plans somehow got mixed up with plans for one of the other two Greenbelt communities (in Ohio and Maryland).

Not so, according to the architect. "We have found much curiosity

> ## *"There is good reason why basements weren't included in the plans..."*

about the fact that the houses have no basements. There is good reason why they were not included in the plans," Harry Bentley explained in a story appearing in the August 20, 1936 *Milwaukee Journal.*

"Progress has made the basement old-fashioned, unnecessary and expensive. We can build more and better above the ground because we are building less underground."

The result, he contended, was

better houses for less money.

At least one resident wanted to have a basement and took matters into his own hands. Truman Seiler, who moved to Greendale in 1946 with his wife, Marian, dug a basement under their home on Cardinal Court and maintains he was the first to do so.

"I dug my basement out by hand, shovelful by shovelful," he said. "It took me 11 months to dig it all out. Once that was done, it took only 1 day to pour the cement for it."

Another story circulating for years was the one about the village's garages having been the "shipping crates" for the homes—that the materials for each home were shipped in a large crate, which was later attached to the house to become the garage.

"That's just not true," says John Kuglitsch, who served as village

MUST BE A MONDAY. Washlines got big use throughout the village. These clothes were sure to be "sun-dried".

manager from 1950 to 1979.

Without television and mass communication in those early years, the village residents obviously enjoyed sharing gossipy tidbits to keep life interesting.

Greendale's building planners didn't foresee what later turned into one major building flaw—damp, sweating and cold floors on the ground levels of the homes. The concrete foundations rested almost directly on farmland, with only about 2 or 3 feet of air space under the floor.

Laid atop the concrete was soft, dark red-colored asphalt tile flooring on which moisture accumulated in the summer because of condensation. The tile was uncomfortably cold in winter, too. There was no such problem with the second floors; they were hardwood.

Chet Moehrlin recalls the discomfort. "The moisture from the ground seeped right though," he says. "Our carpeting would get soggy, and we'd have to drag it outside and hang it on a line to dry."

Eileen Campbell laments, "It was about 20 degrees colder near the floor in the winter. We often had to go upstairs to keep warm."

So, special insulation was blown under the affected foundations, and this largely took care of the dampness and sweating.

John Miller remembers, "They blew in about 2-1/2 inches of chopped newspaper and tar. That kept the concrete floors from sweating and pretty much solved the problem."

But not completely, at least in winter, when electric power outages were frequent. "With so many people using their heaters, there wasn't enough electric power," Eileen explains.

"That happened a lot in those early years," says Evelyn Truppe. "It didn't even have to be a bad storm for the electricity to fail again."

Early Greendale residents got their water from two artesian wells, each about 2,000 feet deep. Each had a pumping station and an elevated storage tank. The water was centrally softened.

Flooding was another threat. The farmland on which Greendale was built was catacombed with a series of drainage tiles that carried water into Dale Creek in the middle of the village.

When rains were particularly heavy, the underground tiles proved inadequate. Water then backed up and tended to collect under the foundations.

This problem was eventually solved, too. A series of special drains was connected to storm sewers, eliminating the standing water under the foundations.

To make sure Greendale's new water mains didn't contribute to the underground seepage, special detection equipment was installed to pinpoint even a minor seepage and set off a vibration that pinpointed the location of the leak. Pretty ingenious for the late 1930s.

The Greendale Review, obviously with tongue in cheek, cautioned residents not to be surprised if they saw Walter Kroening, assistant village manager, "wandering around in the small hours of the night, wearing headphones and muttering mysterious abracadabra. Those quiet hours are the best time to discover any water main leaks."

Aside from the dampness and coldness of the tile floors, Marian Prey had decorator problems with her floors on Blossom Court.

"We weren't allowed to put any flooring in the kitchen. All we could have was something like linoleum, and we couldn't glue it on," she says. "We could only lay it down. Those were the rules."

CARPENTER APPRENTICES posed in 1936. The one with the suit and tilted hat must have been the boss.

CHAPTER 9

No Shortage of 'Advice' from Landlord

LIKE ALL earthly paradises, early Greendale had a few shortcomings. The U.S. Government had rules for its tenants, which were as rigid as any private landlord responsible for total maintenance of the homes. Its list of dos and don'ts covered everything from how to operate the electric stoves to taking out the garbage.

Every new family was quickly acquainted with the rules in a government pamphlet welcoming them to the village. The rules were subtly cloaked as "Helpful Suggestions for Greendale Residents".

To enforce its rules, the government issued periodic admonitions. Residents were reminded, for example, that their leases prohibited changes to either the inside or outside of their homes and yards without the written consent of the government.

The restrictions included what could be done with screens, porches, fences, trellises, vine ladders, awnings, rock gardens, terraces, walks and permanent landscape plantings.

And for those who forgot certain other rules of conduct, the following caution was published in the December 1, 1938 edition of *The Greendale Review*:

"A number of screens are still in place throughout the village. Such screens should be taken down as soon as possible. Leaving them in place will result in early deterioration, undue swelling and warping. The Management cannot be responsible for damage caused to screens due to neglect."

The same edition also carried this warning: "Residents are warned NOT to deposit bottles or glass of any shape or form in the *orange bottom can*. The incinerator was almost wrecked last week by bottles placed in the orange bottom can by unthinking residents."

Advised to Defrost Weekly

The government had plenty of other advice for Greendale housewives on how to run their households, as these suggestions and admonitions, published in the March 11, 1939 edition of *The Greendale Review*, attest:

● "Exterior combination doors must be securely latched at all times. Slightly open doors are easily caught by heavy winds and torn from their hinges. The Management has recently adopted a policy to charge householders for damage due to such negligence."

● "It's best not to keep bananas in the refrigerator. And cucumbers, cooked cabbage, cauliflower, maraschino cherries, strong cheese and pickles should be kept in covered containers or wrapped in waxed paper."

● "Defrosting should be done weekly."

And there was this strong suggestion during the winter months: "Do not use more water than is necessary for dust prevention when putting ashes in your refuse containers. Excess water turns into ice when the cans are set out for collection and causes difficulty in proper removal of the ashes."

What with burning coal and wood for heating, there was a lot of ashes to deal with.

Evelyn Truppe remembers those ashes all too well. "It seems whenever Walter started cleaning the ashes out of the furnace, I'd say to him, 'Do you have to do that right now? Don't. I just scrubbed today.' It was always such a mess," she says.

Ask Jack Murdaugh about the ashes. "I remember taking them out and storing them in a container in the ground.

"To open the lid, you stepped on a handle, then scooped the ashes out of a bucket with a shovel into the container," he explains. "We still have one of those shovels. It was kind of a rough job."

As the initial challenges were gradually overcome, the new Greendalers turned their attention to other pressing matters. Living in an isolated community on the outskirts of an urban area, they quickly learned, would test their ingenuity.

Their diligent and cooperative handling of one priority after another stamped the first 2 years—1938 and 1939—as truly memorable ones in the village's annals. Their actions shaped, perhaps unknowingly at the time, the unique tradition that has characterized Greendale during the first 66 years of its existence as a dynamic yet contented lifestyle.

Responding in true pioneer style a mere 2 months after the first families arrived, the new residents formed a "General Committee" to coordinate all village activities. It, in turn, created subcommittees charged

---

"Living in an isolated community tested their ingenuity…"

---

with tackling the village's critical needs of transportation, communication and medical facilities.

The committee initiated and handled the details of incorporation and relations with the government plus started a credit union.

They also started a labor relations subcommittee to assist unemployed residents and later began a more permanent Citizens Association, which would take over the work of the General Committee on January 1, 1939.

A particularly big early challenge

was transportation, especially as a means of getting back and forth to the big city. There was no public transportation linking Greendale with Milwaukee in the late '30s.

Fathers needed to get to their jobs…mothers needed to do their shopping…children had to attend school.

Only a few families owned cars. Those without vehicles either carpooled or were shuttled to the nearest public bus stop in Milwaukee, 3 miles away. Even then, travel between Greendale and Milwaukee, by whatever means, generally took as long as 2 hours.

The shuttle was a station wagon driven by Bill McFarland, whom everyone called "Old Mac". The service was free and initially available every weekday, early each morning from 5:35 to 7:35 and af-

EARLY PHOTO shows excavating the roadbed for South 76th Street. Apple orchard at right, owned by August Kneser, was east of the street. Note the vintage water wagon and toolbox behind the large steam-driven shovel.

Encounters of the Animal Kind

EARLY GREENDALERS had their share of encounters with animal life around the village.

"First, there was a kind of bug that some called an armyworm, a caterpillar that energetically chewed all the leaves off trees and grass right down to the bare ground," recalls Marian Prey.

The critters invaded Greendale's streets and sidewalks during the summer of 1939.

"They even crawled into our houses and chewed on the carpeting," says Marian. "The government people had to come in and spray, and that eventually got rid of them."

There were also lots of pheasants, raccoons and owls in the neighborhoods. After all, in the '30s,

Greendale was still in the middle of "farm country".

"I remember an owl sitting on our window. It scared the daylights out of me, a city girl living out in the country!" Marian admits.

"Later, when we lived in a townhouse on Basswood Street, we heard a noise one night," she adds. "It was a raccoon that had gotten in through an opening in the foundation of the house. He ran up the stairs and into the bathroom! I think he was looking for a drink of water.

"I called the fire department, and I'm sure they must have thought I'd been at the village tavern and had too much to drink. But they came out and found the raccoon hiding in a corner."

ternoons between 3:05 and 5:05.

Later, a private bus company began service, offering rides to and from downtown Milwaukee every day of the week, starting from Greendale at 7:05 in the morning and arriving back as late as midnight. The fare was 25¢ each way.

In August of 1938, Sherwood Reeder and a government attorney appeared before the Public Service Commission of Wisconsin to petition for public transportation.

In October, the PSC ordered a 6-month trial of regular bus service, and the village's free shuttle service was discontinued. Unfortunately, the bus service trial didn't work out because of what residents contended was a mixture of "poor service and high fares".

Public transportation continued to plague Greendalers for a long time after that, as bus service from several carriers remained intermittent and undependable.

"Getting around" certainly was not easy during the early years. But some pioneers say it was the very problem that brought them closer together and helped them become more neighborly.

STREET SCENES from 1938 show houses along Bramble Court (top) and Greendale's first taxi parked along Northway. Taxi service was needed to get to the bus stop.

ALL SORTS of specialty trades were needed to turn Greendale into a reality. Above, two blacksmiths work in one of the construction sheds along Grange Avenue.

STATELY BUILDING. Below is the Village Hall shortly after completion in May of 1938. Some say it was fashioned after the Governor's Palace at Williamsburg, Virginia.

CHAPTER 10

The Communication Challenge

IF TRANSPORTATION was an early problem, communication was an equal challenge. There were no telephones in the homes. In fact, there were only two phones in the village—one in the police station and the other, a pay phone, in the Village Hall.

To make a call to Hales Corners, the caller had to deposit a nickel in the phone. Calls to Milwaukee were a dime. Phones were installed later in a few homes, but they were temporarily disconnected during World War II.

Dial phone service was introduced in March 1950, and that meant no more toll charges.

Greendale was included in the Milwaukee Telephone District, giving residents local calling access to all greater Milwaukee area numbers. The changeover required doing away with the village's three-digit-plus-a-letter phone numbers and replacing them with two-letter, five-digit phone numbers.

There were no mailboxes on homes in the village's early days. They weren't needed because there was no home mail delivery. There wasn't even bulk mail service to Greendale.

Got Mail from Milwaukee

Bill McFarland, the shuttle driver, drove each day to the main post office in downtown Milwaukee to get the mail for all village residents. He dropped it off at the Village Hall, where it was piled in shoe boxes.

Greendale residents then made it part of their daily routine to walk to the Village Hall for their mail. That proved to be a social blessing in disguise because, as Viola Eilers describes it, "We looked forward to meeting everybody every day. It helped us get acquainted with other folks and gave us a chance to chat as we picked up our mail."

Carol Curtin recalls, "We waited in line, as a lady sitting at a desk near the door called off our

MILK TRUCKS were busy in Greendale. This one was operated by "Doc" Seiler in 1951. Those are his daughters, Kerry, Susie and Pam, in the truck.

names and handed out the mail. It was just like an army mail call."

"We women especially enjoyed meeting at the Village Hall, since no mother could hold a job outside of the home," notes Eileen Campbell. "We certainly got better acquainted with our neighbors."

The Campbells and the Truppes were neighbors. "Eileen and Arnold lived across the street from us on Azalea for a long, long time," Evelyn Truppe says.

"When our first child, Ellen, was born, the day after I came home from the hospital, there was a knock on the door. It was Eileen. She brought her youngest over to sit with us. She said, 'I knew you'd be home alone for the first time today.'

"That's the kind of good neighbors we had," Evelyn says. "We never locked our doors.

"In later years, when we were going to be away when the milkman came, I'd write him a note about what we needed and leave the door unlocked so he could walk in and put the milk in the refrigerator."

The mail situation eventually improved. A fourth-class post office was opened in a building near the Village Inn. Ed Bengs, of Badger Court, was named postmaster and

---

"Going to the post office every day helped us meet people..."

Leo Hoyer, who lived on Dendron Lane, was hired as its first clerk. He later became assistant postmaster when Greendale was designated a first-class facility.

"I got to know everybody," Leo says. "Even the kids came in, two, three times a day to pick up the mail."

CONSTRUCTION SHEDS south of Grange Avenue are where the planning department and various skilled tradesmen did their work.

"We'd go to the window and ask for our mail," explains Carol Curtin. "Only one person was allowed at the mail window at a time. Some people had lockboxes.

"I remember helping out at Christmas, sorting mail every morning," she adds. "I was 16 at the time and got paid $2 a week. I didn't have to take any kind of test for the job."

Finally, an eager 19-year-old started a mail delivery service. "His name was Bill McNaab," Carol says. "He went house to house, asking if people wanted their mail delivered. He charged something like $15 for a year."

While having a delivery service meant residents no longer met neighbors at the post office, they learned they could now send letters to anyone within the village for a penny an ounce. And that they did, since there were still no home phones.

Another way neighbors kept in touch, and were informed about local meetings and social events, was the bulletin board mounted in the Village Hall lobby.

It served as Greendale's first news media until members of the Greendale Journalism Club, with Edith Guyor as acting editor in chief, volunteered to mimeograph 14 pages of news. They called the publication the *Greendale Bulletin*.

The date was August 24, 1938. Within a month, it was renamed *The Greendale Review*, a new title designed by Ruth Owens, and published every other Thursday.

Subsequently, Harold Minnick took over as chairman from Miss

POST OFFICE (below) is where many of the village's early residents got acquainted, since there was no home delivery. Above is Gladys Bengs, wife of Greendale's first postmaster, Ed Bengs.

Guyor, who returned to the Greendale school staff as librarian. Bramble Burke became managing editor, Harold Huber was named editor, and volunteers continued to report local happenings.

With the start of the new year, *The Greendale Review* upped the price of an issue a penny to 5¢. Paid subscriptions were 50¢ for 13 issues, and $1 for 26 issues.

Publication of the *Review* as a community project staffed by volunteers ended the following August, when the newspaper was incorporated as a business organization. Despite the reorganization, *The Greendale Review* remained under community control through a membership arrangement, by which the village's residents elected the board of directors, who were directly responsible to them.

Prehistoric Dam Discovered Near the Village Hall

GREENDALE, according to some accounts, was a camping ground for the Potawatomi Indians about a century before the land's emergence as a Greenbelt Town. A tribal burial ground just north of the Village Hall reportedly was discovered during construction.

As evidence of the Potawatomis' presence in the area, Indian arrowheads have been found in Pioneer Park and other areas of the village as recently as the 1990s. However, the original village site may have been inhabited even before the Potawatomis.

In one of his regular "Across the Manager's Desk" columns in *The Greendale Review*, Community Manager Walter Kroening wrote about workers stumbling across a prehistoric stone dam in the village in 1937. He stated:

"Did you know that a dam exists 25 feet underground directly below the intersection of Angle Lane and Northway? It's true.

"During the construction of the sanitary sewer at the corner of Northway and Angle Lane, a man-made dam of large boulders was discovered at a depth varying from 20 to 25 feet. Geologists hesitated to state its approximate construction date, but it was agreed that it was many centuries ago.

"This 'boulder dam' was the cause of a huge peat bog discovered in the area just north of its location. Over 95,000 cubic yards of peat were removed in the construction of the Angle Lane roadway. This was necessary to prevent future settling of the roadway.

"Further evidence of the dam was discovered at the northeast corner of Municipal Square. It is logical to assume that the original location of Dale Creek was west of its present location, before some prehistoric tribe built the dam to impound its waters."

So, it's entirely likely that Dale Creek originally flowed on the west side of Broad Street.

AERIAL VIEW of blossoming village center was taken on Aug. 5, 1939. Circle indicates location of ancient dam mentioned above. The Village Hall is to its right.

CHAPTER 11

Vendors, Gardens Provided Food

ISOLATED GREENDALERS dealt with the challenge of food shopping in various and resourceful ways. Virginia Fahlhaber and others did their shopping at a local "store on wheels".

"A truck loaded with groceries came around to our homes a couple times a week," Virginia recalls. "The street vendor stocked meat, too, packed in ice to keep it fresh."

He also extended credit. "There were many times he put us in his little book, carrying our bill to the next day or week because we were poor," says Viola Eilers.

In the early days there were lots of street vendors, eager to sell products to residents who lived far from grocery stores. The bakery man, the fruit man and even the ragman peddled goodies from their wagons.

"I remember the ragman; he was from the Old Country and kind of sinister-looking. He scared us," says Judy Birch. "He had an

old truck that moved along like an old Model T. And he would cry out, 'Rex...Rex...Rex!' I finally understood he was saying 'Rags... Rags...Rags!' He also sharpened scissors."

"Then there was the fruit man, who had lots of stuff for canning, from A to Z, on his wagon," recalls Viola. "I canned some 500 jars each year from my garden,

plus I made jams and jellies.

"I also remember the bakery man, a Mr. Johnson. He had the best breads and sweet rolls and pastries."

Evelyn Truppe agrees: "The bakery man came two or three times a week. He'd blow his horn, and everyone would come flying out to buy his sweet goods.

"We also bought meat from a

GREENDALE earned its title of "The Garden Community" early, as evidenced by flowers among homes.

man who came around with a truck," says Evelyn. "And there was another little man who sold vegetables. He fascinated me. We'd buy from him; he'd put it in a bag, then write the prices on the bag and add them up real fast. I'd go home and check his prices, and he was always right, even though I couldn't add them up that fast."

Roots of Garden Community

Many early residents grew a great deal of their foodstuffs, turning their large backyards into gardens. This tendency toward having large gardens, both vegetable and flower, led to the label the village proudly carries today: "Greendale—The Garden Community" (see more in Chapter 29).

Eileen and Arnold Campbell were typical gardeners. "We grew more than just vegetables. We grew strawberries, red raspberries and pumpkins," says Eileen. "We also picked wild raspberries from a nearby woods.

"I canned about 18 quarts of raspberries one year and saved some fresh ones for nibbling. We stored them in the sub-area under our utility room where it was cooler."

Ellis Brown recalls the garden in back of his home on Basswood Street: "I started with tomatoes and pepper plants and later added beans and carrots."

Marian Prey's big home garden and numerous fruit trees in her yard kept her busy canning. "Along with all the vegetables in our garden, our trees yielded pears, apples and plums.

"I especially remember the ap-

"The bakery man blew his horn, and everyone would come flying out to buy his sweet goods…"

---

ple tree. My husband, Stanley, picked apples each season, using an apple picker he ingeniously made out of a coffee can and a bamboo fishing pole. A fruit man from Milwaukee bought the apples from us for a dollar a bushel."

Greendale's housewives were proud of their food canning achievements. A village fair—the first of many over those early years—was held in the Community Building in September 1938, a mere 4 months after the first families arrived.

The Greendale Review reported, "Greendale housewives did themselves proud with their show of canned goods."

The second year, the fair became known as the Annual Greendale Fair, "for the exhibition and judging of flowers and other garden produce, hobbies and handicrafts."

"It was like a small state fair," recalls Eleanor Jolly.

A Garden Club was formed, too, and it arranged for the judging and awarding of ribbon prizes. By the time the third annual event rolled around, other types of exhibits were being encouraged, such as clothing, home furnishings, and table settings for formal and informal dinners.

VEGETABLE GARDENS came first with pioneers, but flowers were a close second, even planted amid rocks.

PLANTING TIME. Jeanette Des Jardin and son Kendall get ready to start their spring garden with wagonload of plants.

BACKYARDS became small "vegetable farms" (below) as pioneer residents produced much of their own food.

WIRE FENCING separated backyards behind small "Honeymoon Cottages" (above) looking east toward Angle Lane.

ROCK GARDENS separated lots (below). Houses were placed close to the street to allow for spacious backyards.

CHAPTER 12

Co-operatives Were a Success

FINDING A DAILY milk supply was another kind of adventure. Virginia Fahlhaber walked each day to get her supply direct from the cows at the neighboring Van Alstine farm on South 76th Street, along the western edge of the village, now the site of Our Shepherd Lutheran Church.

Viola Eilers and her neighbors, on the other hand, organized a "milk pail pool".

"Each day, someone collected 2-gallon pails with our names on them and got the milk from Tom Van Alstine's place," she explains. "Although the milk wasn't pasteurized," Viola adds, "we never got sick. We sifted it through some fine sheeting."

The government quickly put a halt to that. "We got a notice that we were not supposed to use that milk since it wasn't pasteurized

"MILK PAIL POOL" was organized by residents who took turns going to the nearby Van Alstine farm for milk. Below, Village Manager Walter Kroening talks with Tom Van Alstine in 1941.

53

WHITEY MAGNON serves a customer at village's co-op grocery in 1939. Note those enviable prices above counter!

and there was the danger of getting what they called 'undulant fever'," says Virginia.

"I wasn't worried, of course, because I was born and raised on a farm, and we'd always drank unpasteurized milk. But anyway, we stopped buying it there until they put in pasteurizing equipment."

Eileen Moss stated her preference for raw milk in a letter to the editor of the *Review*, urging fellow residents to defeat a pending village ordinance requiring that milk from surrounding farms be pasteurized.

"People are beginning to realize that when milk is pasteurized, not only the disease and unfriendly germs are killed, but also the friendly and health-giving bacteria," she wrote. "For that reason, it has far less nutritional value than raw milk.

"I would like to ask this pertinent question: Why aren't all the farmers dead? They've been drinking raw milk since they were mere babies."

On the contrary, two cases of undulant fever were traced by state health officials to local drinking of raw milk, and it wasn't long before pasteurizing equipment was installed on the Van Alstine farm.

Soon after, a consumer's dairy co-op was formed by five village residents, Raymond Miller, Harold Wylie, Herman Jennrich, Thomas Byrnes and Edward Stettler.

Membership in the Greendale Dairy Co-operative Association cost $1 to cover the cost of milk bottles. Consisting of some 150 families, it was divided into "rings" of eight to 12 families each. Members within each ring took turns collecting the milk from the village's farms and took it to the pasteurizing plant at Van Alstine's.

Co-op members needed to come up with a system that determined how much of a dividend was due from each member. They decided to simply have each member turn in their bottle caps. This system worked well—it was estimated the members would end up paying about 18¢ less per gallon than Milwaukee households paid.

Another Co-op Formed

All the residents' efforts to put food on the table prompted the innovative creation of another co-operative, one that would give them access to food and utility products at wholesale prices.

Within a space of several weeks, the Greendale Co-operative Association was organized. On August

22, 1938, two committee members, Delbert Engel and Alois Washkowiak, traveled to Madison to file the papers legalizing the association. (Similar co-op associations were already operating successfully in the other two Greenbelt Towns.)

Greendale's Co-operative Association entered into a 10-year arrangement with the U.S. Department of Agriculture, allowing it to manage and operate all business enterprises in the village, including a self-service food store, gas station and garage, drugstore, barbershop and theatre.

Subsequently, the Co-op's board of directors decided to lease the drugstore, variety store and theatre to private individuals. The Co-op agreed to pay normal rental fees for the commercial properties based on a percentage of the gross sales of the various businesses.

All residents of Greendale were given the opportunity to participate in the ownership and management of the association, with all profits from its operation of the retail stores benefiting the residents.

"Pressure" to Join Co-op

In an editorial dated September 23, 1938, *The Greendale Review* urged residents to become owners in the Co-operative:

"A Co-operative is controlled by its members. Everything above the cost and operating expense is returned to you. Your money and your patronage will help make it successful. You can buy one or more shares at $15 each, or you can begin buying a share with a reasonable down payment. It's like financing your own business."

Many Greendalers heeded the advice. The Co-operative's food store was opened that November with Ed Van Ess, who lived on Apple Court, as manager. The store was in the Mercantile Building, today the site of the Greendale Public Library.

The food store's initial bargains included four tall cans of milk for 25¢; a 3-pound can of coffee, 43¢; 14-ounce bottle of ketchup, 10¢; 24-1/2-pound bag of wheat flour, 59¢; round steak for 30¢ a pound; sirloin steaks, 32¢ a pound; T-bone steaks, 35¢ a pound; fresh ground meat, 21¢ a pound; and leg of lamb, 26¢ a pound.

As low as those prices may sound these days, they didn't please everyone, considering the nation was still in the grip of the Great Depression. To meet objections and cut costs, prices were lowered on many items, credit was extended and self-service was introduced.

To further promote patronage of

READY TO OPEN. Self-service was encouraged at grocery, and shoppers could put their bill "on the tab".

THIS GAS STATION, operated as another co-op, was located at the corner of Parking Street and Northway. Photo was taken in May 1939.

the store, it was suggested that street peddlers be forced to obtain licenses to limit or eliminate their presence in the village.

The Co-op Association considered that step too extreme. The same purpose could be accomplished "by making the shopping center so attractive that people will not care to patronize outside enterprises."

Not all Greendale families felt the need to belong to the Co-op. Among them were the parents of George Weimer, who lived on one of the farms surrounding the village's residential sections.

Their large farm extended along both sides of South 51st Street, from West Grange Avenue down to Scout Lake, and east to South 43rd and Ramsey Streets.

"My parents rented the land from the government and did dairy farming there," George notes. "They also raised hogs, chickens and cows and even had horses. They really didn't need the Co-op because they raised everything themselves."

In quick order that first year, the Co-operative opened a "Super Service" gas station, promising a full line of auto accessories. It was managed by Ray Almquist.

Within the next 18 months, the gas station was being hailed as a success. Of the 415 cars registered

in the village, 400 were patronizing the station. The sales volume helped fatten the cash dividend rebate that each Co-op member received at the end of each fiscal year.

While the Co-op was proving successful, a story making the rounds was that Ray was using "soft arm" tactics to sign up members in the Co-op. He approached six of his friends at the village's second

> ## *"The barber gave free haircuts to families short on funds…"*

anniversary dance and asked for a dollar, according to the story in *The Greendale Review*.

"Thinking he was in an embarrassed financial position, they gladly handed him the money. 'Fine,' said Almquist. 'You are now a member of the Co-op; you have 2 whole years to pay the rest.' In spite of the fact that it was so unexpected, none of the six reneged on the deal."

The Co-operative opened a barbershop that year, leasing it to Archie "Red" McCosh. He was, according to one anonymous admirer, "a silver-tongued orator barber". Assisting him was Orville Harris.

Both men had some 17 years of barbering experience, and both were Greendale residents.

The announcement of the barbershop opening included this reassuring appeal to female residents: "You women folks will be glad to know that both barbers are specialists in women's hairstyles as well."

As for the men, the announcement encouraged them to "Come in and get your ears lowered."

"I remember sending my sons, Warner and Gary, to Red for their haircuts," notes Eleanor Jolly. "I'd give them a dollar bill. Seventy cents was for the two haircuts, and 15¢ apiece for a hot fudge sundae at the Des Jardins' drugstore."

For quite a number of village residents, paying for their children's haircuts was a hardship. Sensitive to the plight of unemployed breadwinners in these families, McCosh on several occasions offered to give free haircuts to their children under the age of 14.

"You are showing the true 'Greendale Spirit'," proclaimed *The Greendale Review* in its story about his generous offer.

CHAPTER 13

One-Room School for Eight Grades

WELL BEFORE Greendale's beginning, there was a one-room brick building on the northeast corner of South 76th Street and West Grange Avenue (which was named Center Street back then).

It was called the Spring Hill School. Roger Klett speculates the schoolhouse was built sometime between 1870 and 1880.

The school was still there, part of School District 13 in the Town of Greenfield, when the first tenants were moving into Greendale. One teacher taught kindergarten through eighth grade. Most of the pupils were children from area farms.

For a time, Rose Basse was the teacher, juggling all subjects in all grades. "When she and Dad got married, she had to quit," says Ruth (Basse) Klussendorf. "Back then, women weren't allowed to continue teaching after they were married."

The pupil population of the school would be the envy of a teacher today. Total enrollment in all eight grades numbered approximately 20.

"There were only three in my class from first grade on," observes Ruth, "and there was only one girl in the grade above mine."

Ruth's brother Robert, 3 years younger, was also a student there. Her brother Alvin was an infant at the time.

The Basse farm was located on the south side of Grange Avenue, between 60th and 76th Streets. When it was purchased by the government in June of 1936, the farm became the center of Green-

SPRING HILL SCHOOL, built in late 1800s, was on northeast corner of 76th and Grange. It closed in 1938.

Jiggs

DOGS likely weren't allowed at Spring Hill School regularly, so maybe this was "Bring Your Pet Day". Ruth Basse, whose family's farm was nearby, is the happy girl at far right.

ENTIRE STUDENT BODY of Spring Hill School poses in 1935 on what must have been a cold winter day. Today, a Speedway service station is at this site at 76th and Grange.

dale. Ruth and Robert then left the school, moving with their parents to a farm near Muskego, a few miles to the west. In the time-consuming move, they hauled much of their machinery and livestock on farm wagons pulled by horses and tractors.

The teacher in the school's last school year, 1937-38, was Miss Evelyn Shebel, whose annual salary was $945.

John Miller holds personal memories of the old schoolhouse. "After the building was abandoned, we used to hold Scout meetings there. It became our clubhouse in 1938," John says.

"We'd been told no one could buy the building because it was built as a school, and it had to stay that way or the property would go back to the original owner."

Harry Brandt Jr. was the first scoutmaster and John Burnham served as committee chairman. The troop consisted of 27 Scouts.

Not to be outdone, 27 Greendale girls became Girl Scouts at an investiture ceremony in March. Designated as Troop 99, they wasted no time building up their treasury. They sold 410 dozen Girl Scout cookies and netted another $20 selling Christmas cards.

Russell LaRose has fond memories of using the empty schoolhouse as a "hangar" to rebuild a small airplane. "An Air Scout group that I belonged to used the old schoolhouse for our plane project," he says.

Roger Klett remembers that proj-

ect well, too. "We bought the plane —a Piper Cub J3, which was in need of repair—in St. Louis. It cost us $180. We each chipped in $18," he says.

"Paul Schroeter went to St. Louis and somehow flew it back here. We managed to roll it into the schoolhouse because the doors were wide enough, and the plane's body and wings were quite narrow.

"We spent many a night in that

"The annual salary of the teacher was $945..."

---

schoolhouse, re-covering the wings and body with canvas, spraying it with paint and getting giddy from the fumes," Roger recalls.

Jack Murdaugh observed the plane overhaul. "I remember looking through the schoolhouse windows and wondering what was going on inside. I wasn't involved in it," he says, "but it fascinated me. I don't know if it ever got off the ground," he adds.

Roger says it did. "The group got to fly the plane. That was around 1951. But I didn't, because about that time I went into the service," he laments. "I don't know whatever happened to that plane," Roger wonders. "I probably still own one-tenth of it."

In any event, the schoolhouse was torn down sometime during the 1950s, and the site was taken over

by the Clarence Welk service station. Today it's a Speedway gas station/convenience store.

Sculpture Still Stands

One enduring reminder of Greendale from its very beginnings still stands on its original site. It's the unique flagpole and sculpture set in a limestone base, just east of Greendale Middle School.

It was sculpted by Alonzo Hauser, a graduate of the Layton School of Art in Milwaukee. The WPA had launched a nationwide program to provide work for professional artists during this period of major housing construction.

Hauser was commissioned by the WPA "to create an artwork that would depict the kind of people who'd make up an ideal community." His talent proved worthy of the task.

The flagpole's five-sided limestone base is 12 feet high and 5 feet wide. It weighs 8 tons. Hauser hand-carved figures that represented families, young people, laborers and farmers—all typical of the people who chose to become pioneers in a new way of urban life.

One news report has it that funds ran out after he had done the initial work, and that Hauser accepted the pay of a WPA laborer to finish it. At any rate, the project took him 6 months to complete.

BASSE FARM was along south side of Grange Avenue, about where the American Legion building is now.

ALONZO HAUSER created the statue at foot of village flagpole and also the relief artwork (above) at Greendale Middle School. Note the hanging lights for the tennis courts, which were located near the statue.

CHAPTER 14

Community Emergency Services Needed

THE GOVERNMENT started a number of new projects to benefit early Greendale residents. First was the National Youth Administration project (NYA), an experimental farm designed to teach youngsters agriculture and landscaping. Greendale was chosen as one of 10 NYA resident centers for boys and two centers for girls in Wisconsin.

The new NYA resident center was located on Loomis Road near the Root River, on about 8 acres in a section of land that was still rural. It consisted of two houses, a

FIRST POLICE FORCE was assembled in 1936 to provide security during construction phase. This building was among temporary construction sheds.

VILLAGE'S FIRST FIRE TRUCK takes part in Fourth of July parade on Broad Street with volunteer firefighters.

barn and a garage. One house served as a dormitory for 23 youths.

The young men, ages 18 to 25 and drawn from counties throughout the state, worked 54 hours a month doing landscape work. This work was formerly handled by the Works Progress Administration (WPA). They also shared housekeeping duties, cooking meals and keeping their dorm in order.

Next on Greendale's early agenda was the need for community emergency services—notably fire, police and medical.

Up until then, police protection was the responsibility of one person—Alois Werner, who also served as village constable. He quickly added four officers, whose main duties were patrolling the village to protect new residents and building materials.

In 1939, the village organized a Department of Public Safety, composed of both the police and fire personnel. Robert Taylor came from Wichita, Kansas to head the new department. He was succeeded by Harold Bruett 3 years later.

A reporter for *The Greendale Review* commented that Chief Bruett, being 6 feet 2-1/2 inches tall, "should have no trouble being seen in a crowd."

Bruett served the community until 1971, a total of 29 years, the longest tenure of Greendale's four police chiefs. Myron Ratkowski then took over and served 14 years, until 1985. He was succeeded by David J. Leack. Robert Dams now heads the department.

The building, which still stands at Schoolway and Parking Street, once

> *"At 6 feet 2-1/2 inches tall, Chief Bruett should be seen in any crowd…"*

housed both the police and fire agencies. In 1968, fire department personnel were moved to new, separate quarters at Southway and Loomis, freeing up the old building for expanded police operations.

The police department moved to

its own larger headquarters when the Greendale Safety Center was built on the south side of Grange Avenue, between Northway and Loomis. Dedicated on November 12, 1998, the building also includes a courtroom.

Firefighters Paid by the Call

The first fire department was composed of 28 volunteers. Warren Hale was appointed acting fire chief, and Jack Oberhofer was named assistant chief. The other men were organized into two companies of 12 men each, one working the day shift, the other the night shift.

The department relied on volunteer firemen until May 1965, when it hired three full-time firefighters and Arthur Orlowski as full-time chief. Others heading the department included Arnold Heling, James Strange and Gary Fedder, the current police chief.

Art Krueger says he was one of the volunteer firemen, but not for long. "Even though the siren was a block away from our house on Carnation Court, I could never hear it because I slept so soundly," Art confesses. "So I told 'em they'd better not have a fireman who can't hear the siren."

George Weimer lasted a lot longer. "I served as a volunteer fireman for 24 years; Harry Brandt was chief then," he says. "We were paid by the call. Sometimes when I'd have to answer a call in the middle of the night, I'd get back just in time to go to work in the morning."

The department's first fire truck was a converted 1921 Ford Model T truck. Its equipment consisted of a two-cycle engine, which could only spray about 70 gallons of water a minute through a 1-inch hose. Such "firepower" could barely soak a lawn, much less douse a fire.

It wasn't long before the department acquired a "spanking-new" fire truck, capable of pumping up to 700 gallons of water through a 2-1/2-inch hose. The new truck attracted a lot of attention from fire buffs, and fire officials felt it necessary to remind residents that, by law, only firemen could be aboard the

First Fire Chief Warren Hale

truck when it responded to alarms.

Some of the early fires in the village didn't amount to much, but they provided good training for the volunteer firefighters.

In one of their first calls, the volunteers encountered a burning tree stump at the corner of Northway and Arrowwood. *The Greendale Review's* account of the blaze sounded dismissive:

"Although anyone would have been able to douse the fire with a pail of water, the fire alarm sounded, and firemen came hurrying from all directions to answer the call."

Then there was the pea soup fire. Karen Fogelberg says she was responsible for that one.

"Mother was working at the Co-op store and had told me that when I got home from school, I should check on a pot of pea soup she'd put on the stove," she recounts.

"Well, I didn't go right home. I stopped to talk with a friend, Jerry Lipko, who was in the grade ahead of me. Suddenly we saw the fire truck racing past, and Jimmy Owens, who was in my class, charged by on his bicycle, yelling, 'Karen, the fire's at your house!'

"I ran home as quickly as I could, just in time to see the firemen throw

COMBINATION FACILITY housing the police and fire station plus heating plant opened in 1939. Large doors on south side were for fire truck access. Tall smokestack juts above the plant that heated the downtown buildings.

the pot of pea soup out on our lawn.

"The joke at school for a long time after that was 'Who on earth would ever marry Karen? She couldn't even take care of a container of pea soup!' "

A serious fire soon tested the department's capability. It was the fire that destroyed an old barn near Loomis Road and Southway on Saturday, August 5, 1939.

A newly installed siren sounded the alarm, but the fire—which started in straw—quickly consumed the dried lumber of the barn. Firemen controlled the fire and kept it from spreading to several nearby sheds, but the barn was totaled.

History Went Up in Smoke

Another fire that had an emotional impact on village residents was the one that destroyed a big barn located at what is now an extension of the original Clover Lane. With it was lost a very personalized visual account of early Greendale history.

Erwin Koenigsreiter, the manager of Greendale's first and only movie theatre, enjoyed taking amateur movies of various festive occasions in the village.

"He filmed kids' birthday parties, our little parades, the Fourth of July, all the get-togethers we had, the dances and so forth," remembers Bill Henrichs. "Erwin filmed them all and then showed the films later at the theatre."

"He ran them with the newsreel at the Sunday show," adds John Miller. "He stored all those films in that big barn on Clover Lane. And they were all lost in that fire."

Along with the films, the barn housed Erv Trudell's brush cleaner business. Technically, his was the first company in Greendale.

Early Greendalers vividly recall the very day those films were lost to posterity in the blaze—it was January 21, 1949. The disaster was also costly, estimated at $18,000.

"It was terrible," John Miller says sadly. "No one knows exactly how the fire started. I do know a lot of Greendale's history went up in smoke that day."

"I think it was spontaneous combustion," speculates Viola Eilers. "Erwin had rolls and rolls and rolls of film stored in that barn."

Bill Henrichs recalls more details. "Part of the barn was used by a paint company to store containers of flammable liquids used to clean paintbrushes. I think that's where the fire started."

Then there was the December fire at the Howard Schleichert broiler ranch, at the old Chris Beierle homestead on the south end of the village.

"The Greendale fire laddies fought diligently to keep the blaze from spreading to the home," according to the news story in *The Greendale Review*, "but they were too late to save the chicken house."

That "spanking-new" fire truck is long gone, but the tall tower next to the old police garage is still there. "That's where the firemen hung the canvas fire hoses to dry after each fire," says Judy Birch.

Also surviving the years is the building adjacent to the tower, which served as a garage housing all the village's service vehicles. At one time it housed the Youth Center as well.

BARN FIRE at end of Clover Lane had serious repercussions—films of early village events stored in the barn were lost, erasing a visual account of Greendale's history from 1938 to 1949.

CHAPTER 15

Residents Really Trusted Each Other

WHEN PEOPLE applied for jobs in the late 1930s, they didn't go through extensive interviews or need references as they do today. A good example is Art Krueger, who found it easy to become one of Greendale's first policemen.

"A friend of mine called me and said, 'Art, there's a job opening in the police department out here.'

"I replied, 'Well, I didn't graduate from high school. I heard you have to have a high school education to work on a police force.'

"He said, 'No, I don't think so. Come on down. I'll take you in to see Chief Bruett.'

"So we went in and my friend said, 'Harold, here's a good man for you.'

"Chief Bruett looked at me, then said, 'Okay.' That was it. I signed an application and became a policeman in one day. That night, I went around the village with a policeman by the name of George Hart, and the next night I was on my own.

"I rode in the village's squad car. It was a Chevrolet. The village could only afford one.

"I had to cover a lot of area—from 92nd to 43rd Streets, and Edgerton to Highway 36—a lot of streets, a lot of farms and a lot of open spaces," Art recalls.

"I had very few problems in Greendale because there was hardly any crime there. It was the outsiders who kept me busy, like speeders, driving by or through the village.

"The first ticket I handed out was a warning ticket to a fellow going 35 miles an hour in a 20-mph limit. As I pulled him over, he didn't know it, but I was shaking like a leaf. Fortunately, he took the ticket graciously."

Art soon found his job as policeman entailed more than keeping an eye out for crime.

"I remember one time Earl Barr's wife came down to the station and said her kids were jumping on their bed and broke it. She asked if I'd take a look at it.

"I went up to her house and found one of the bed's side bars was broken off. I fixed it with a couple of screws.

"Another time, Ceil Hensley, our village nurse, took me to the house of a woman who was seldom home and wasn't taking good care of her kids," Art re-

Honest Neighbors

THIS ITEM, reprinted verbatim, appeared in the May 29, 1940 issue of *The Greendale Review*:

"While walking down Schoolway, May 17, Mrs. Sam Geracie, 5726 Clover Lane, and Mrs. Harvey Kaeshammer, 5722 Beaver Court, found $75 in bills in front of 6322 Schoolway.

"The money was immediately turned in at the police station, and was later called for by John Spratler, 6322 Schoolway. The $75 was lost by Mrs. Spratler while making a call on a neighbor.

"Phew! Quite a relief, getting the money back, wasn't it, John? Nice to have honest neighbors."

OFFICER ART KRUEGER chats with the Glynn family. (Our staff not only learned names of the people—Sharon, Gary, Tom, baby Pat and Mom Vicky—but the dog's name: "Tubby".)

calls sadly. "They were dirty and needed a bath. It was winter, and the house was ice cold. I checked the furnace and found ashes piled clear up to the grate.

"So I cleaned it all out, made a fire, heated water and gave the kids a bath, then fed them. Sometimes things like that were all part of a day's work back then."

Art's most notable accomplishment as a policeman, however, was entertaining Greendale's youngsters in a special way during the height of the polio scare in the '50s. Viola Eilers recalls that the children had been ordered by the police to stay in their own yards and avoid contact with one another.

"So Art drove up and down the village's streets almost every day, telling stories that he broadcast through a loudspeaker," she says. "We'd sit on the curb, listening to

him as he came down our street."

"He did that on his own, to entertain us kids because we couldn't go anywhere during that quarantine," maintains Bill Henrichs.

The polio quarantine complicated a medical situation in the Krueger household. "We had four daughters at the time, and they needed to have their tonsils taken out," explains Art's wife, Leona. "Dr. Brown couldn't do the operations in the hospital because it was quarantined.

"So he came over and operated on our girls on our dining room table. The operation was a success, but we had four sad little girls on our hands that night."

Husband-and-Wife Team

The general lack of medical services ended during that first summer with the announcement that two doctors—a husband-and-wife team —would be setting up a local med-

ical practice. Dr. Harold Dvorak and his wife, Dr. Laura Fisher, were chosen by the village's Medical Subcommittee, with input from a government representative of the Farm Security Administration.

The doctors generally held office hours from 2 to 4 o'clock in the afternoon, and from 7 to 8 in the evening. All other times were by appointment. They also made house calls, and Dr. Fisher supervised the school's health program.

The village management worked out a fee schedule with the two doctors: $1 for ordinary office calls, $2 for daytime house calls, $3 for nighttime house calls. More extensive services would be extra.

The following January, they joined the village's dentist, Dr. Lomas, in a suite of offices on the second floor of the building housing the post office.

The building was connected by an arcade to the tavern on the north and to the theatre on the south. Dr. Lomas had been chosen from about a half dozen applicants by the Dental Subcommittee.

Because there was no gas service in Greendale's homes, special gas lines—connected to acetylene tanks—had to be installed in the doctors' offices so they could heat their test tubes over an open flame.

The Medical Subcommittee undertook still another important assignment—exploring the possibility of a prepaid group medical service (an early form of an HMO, if you will). The Medical Society of Milwaukee offered a voluntary, prepaid medical and surgical plan with a free choice of some 300 doctors. Each subscriber to the plan would pay the first $24 of medical charges

each year, and the rest of any medical services would be free.

The Medical Subcommittee rejected the society's proposal and recommended instead that a branch facility of the Milwaukee Medical Center be established in Greendale. For this service, each subscriber would pay a monthly fee of $3 per

---

"The doctor often accepted chickens and home-baked bread for pay…"

---

family, $2 a couple and $1 per single person.

The following March, the Milwaukee Medical Center opened a branch facility in Greendale. Within a month, the Greendale Health Association was organized to provide formal cooperation with Milwaukee in administering medical services for villagers. Merrill Burke was the association's chairperson.

The Medical Society of Milwau-

kee's competing plan continued to draw the interest of a number of Greendalers. They soon formed the Greendale Medical Union to support the society's prepaid plan.

Under the plan, a subscriber would pay $1 per month per family, 75¢ for husband and wife and 50¢ for a single person. A subscriber would pay no more than $24 a year in doctor bills. Amounts higher than that would be paid out of a general fund. A minimum of 200 subscribers was required.

Enough residents were interested, and the plan was put into effect that November. Residents now had a choice of two prepaid medical plans.

Jim Curtin remembers his father, Dr. Joseph J. Curtin, coming to Greendale with the opening of the Milwaukee Medical Center office. "Dad's brother was one of the cen-

VILLAGE'S first Chief of Police, Harold Bruett, supervises kids crossing Broad Street and Schoolway in 1939. The large barn at end of Clover Lane is still visible in background at this stage.

ter's founders," says Jim, "and he asked Dad if he'd come out here.

"Dad did. He'd leave at 7 in the morning to make house calls. Then he would have office hours in the afternoon. For an emergency house call, he'd go out any time, day or night.

"He charged $2 for a house call, but many times he accepted payment in the form of chickens or loaves of home-baked bread. Money was not all that plentiful then."

During World War II, the center closed its Greendale office because of the shortage of physicians. Still, emergency calls to the Milwaukee office were responded to within a half hour. Non-emergency calls for service during the daytime had to be made before 8 o'clock in the morning, and before 4 in the afternoon for treatment that evening.

SQUAD CAR, the second one village owned, had two-way radio. Police Chief Harold Bruett stands by Pontiac in '47.

Underground Tunnel Heats Stores

ANOTHER RELIC of the beginning of Greendale is the underground heating tunnel, which to this day still extends from the old police and fire station all the way to the Village Hall.

Big enough to walk through, it served as the central heat source for all the village's public buildings—the Community Building, all the stores on Broad Street and the Village Hall.

At one point, this centralized community heating plant—just west of the police building—consumed some 225 tons of fuel a month to keep all the buildings heated. The tall smokestack of this building is clearly visible in early pictures (see example on page 63), and a shortened version remains today.

The coal was stored underground under the big concrete platform of the heating plant. "Trucks would pull up to the manholes on the platform and dump their loads of coal," recalls John Miller.

"All the kids knew about the tunnel," says Dick Lenten, who admits exploring it a couple of times. "We'd go through it as far as the grating in the police station, which is where the boiler room was," he recounts. "Boy, it was hot in that tunnel."

"It was spooky down there," adds Judy Birch. "We weren't supposed to go in there, but we did anyway."

The water was heated and then circulated all the way to the Village Hall and back, heating all the buildings en route like a huge radiator.

CHAPTER 16

Lots of Reasons to 'Get Together'

GATHERINGS IN people's homes—or "neighborhood get-togethers" as they were called—became a tradition during Greendale's "small town" days, especially during the holiday season. As evidence are these two social items from *The Greendale Review*:

"The Acorn Court residents (all six families) have been entertaining quite lavishly during the holidays. The Schweers had the whole court over at their home on December 26 for lunch and refreshments. The group then had coffee and cookies at the Irvines. The Donnellys and the Silkeys had them all over on the evening of January 1."

And: "The Beaverites (the nickname for those living on Beaver Court) got together for their annual Christmas party at the Cliff Bowens home. After the usual exchange of gifts, there followed a delicious lunch. From what they say, only one court resident was absent on account of an attack of the grippe."

Dick Lenten still remembers a block party during the big snowstorm of 1947. "All the neighbors got together and shoveled out our street. It ended up as sort of a party because as we went along, we kept getting invited in for hot wine," he says.

"By the time we got to the end of the street, everyone felt quite good. But there was a *lot* of snow. We piled it up at one end of our street, then someone stuck a Christmas tree on top of it."

The Community Building was the hub for all organized civic, social and religious activities. It was also home to the village's first school and first library.

Its popularity as a gathering place for residents is attested to in this appeal in *The Greendale Review*: "If you've often wondered what to do with your extra wire clothes hangers, bring them down to the Community Building. This will help to speed up the checking

EVERYONE pitched in to clear side streets after huge snowstorm in 1947.

CHANCES are good that this car over-heated when stuck in deep snowdrifts.

facilities at the next Greendale social event."

The village inspired a great number and variety of organized clubs for fun and for betterment of the community. One estimate had the count at more than 60, and that did not include card clubs and neighborhood groups. Some have survived to this day.

There was even a Men's Forum, formed "to stimulate and create interest in the doings of Greendale for the benefit of its citizens".

Its women's auxiliary, known as the Ladies Forum, later became the Varietee Club, so named for the variety of local activities in which its members were involved.

One of the group's memorable efforts was a Gay Nineties review called "Memory Lane". The community variety show was presented at the Community Building in May of 1941. According to the *Review*, "Greendalers showed off their individual talents in every facet of the musical production."

There was also a Gay Nineties Club, made up of talented young

WORKING TOGETHER to clear snow helped neighbors get acquainted.

GAY NINETIES REVIEW held in 1941 not only helped "bonding" but offered an opportunity to display talents.

mothers and housewives—singers, dancers and musicians. They entertained at various village functions, and, as their reputation spread, were invited to perform at events in outlying areas.

The HARPS Club was a strictly social organization open to residents who claimed Irish heritage. Or, as Jim Kendellen put it, "including everyone who ever met or even knew an Irishman."

Members of the Boots and Saddle Riding Club met at George Nichols' Parkway Ranch on 92nd Street, south of Grange Avenue.

The Greendale Businessmen's Association was represented by Koenigsreiter, Des Jardin, McCosh, Almquist, Bengs, Lomas, Fred Staub, George Olsheske and Edgar Owens of *The Greendale Review*.

A Parent-Teacher Club was organized in 1944, and the Greendale Pioneers' Club, for the earliest settlers, started in May 1945.

With all the overlapping schedules of these social and business clubs, it was bound to happen: The informal gatherings placed competing demands on everyone's free time.

One "meeting-challenged" resident unburdened himself or herself

---

"I should go to the meetings, but I like to dance, too..."

---

in this plaintive letter to the *Review* on February 11, 1939:

"I wonder how many residents of Greendale have been faced with this same perplexing problem. Now, which meeting shall I attend?

"Tonight, there is a regular tenants' meeting, the Co-op Board has a meeting, there's a Village Board meeting scheduled and there's going to be a community dance.

IT'S OBVIOUS a lot of handwork went into clearing this entrance. That sign at left stated the truth for a while!

"I sit and argue with myself; I know I can't divide the time between the two meetings. I've tried it and it just isn't successful. I didn't get a clear picture of what's going on in either place.

"There are some important problems coming up at these boards, which, as a resident, I should take an interest in. But I'd like to go to the dance, too.

"Tuesday night I planned to stay at home and do some of that reading that I've been neglecting. But there was another slip at my door: 'Important meeting tonight, please be present.'

"Shall I go, shall I stay at home. Which meeting should I attend, or should I wait to read about it in *The Greendale Review*?"

—Signed, WONDERING

LOCAL MUSICALS offered low-cost entertainment and provided an outlet for the ample talent of village residents. Elaborate costumed one above was held in Community Building.

TITLE of musical performed by the costumed cast below in 1938 was "Princess, Pigs and Paranoics". It was directed by Myrtle Ross—she's wearing bib overalls in front row.

CHAPTER 17

Residents Decide to Incorporate

UNDERSCORING the rapid establishment of vital and social services in the village was the need to create a community identity anchored in a self-governing system.

As it stood from the beginning, the U.S. Government owned Greendale, but the village was subject to two governing jurisdictions, the Town of Greenfield and the Town of Franklin.

Under growing local pressure, the government agreed to allow residents to decide whether or not they wanted to incorporate, and also what type of governing system they preferred.

On August 4, 1938, barely 3 months after the first tenants had moved in, a group of 10 residents formalized their intent and filed a petition to incorporate Greendale as a village.

The petition was granted in September. In October, residents voted 312 to 142 in favor of incorporating. On November 1, 1938, the Greendale community officially became the Village of Greendale.

The bureaucratic process dictated that residents next elect a slate of officers. In December, George Brinkman, a much-admired local gentleman, was voted in as the village's first president. The position paid him a grand total of $6.25 a month.

Brinkman's dedicated efforts on behalf of Greendale during his tenure earned him the honor of having the village's recreational area south of Broad Street named after him following his untimely

---

"The first village president was paid $6.25 a month…"

---

death on June 26, 1941, at age 53. Still today, Greendale High School's athletic field is called Brinkman Memorial Field.

The field was dedicated in a colorful ceremony highlighted by a parade down Broad Street. Participating were local and neighboring American Legion posts, village officials, civic group representatives and the village's Scouting organizations.

Village President Raymond Miller dedicated the Brinkman Memorial—a bronze plaque mounted on a boulder. The program included music by the Village Band, songs by the Legion Junior Auxiliary, and songs and poems by the village's schoolchildren.

The Greendale Review, in an editorial, referred to George Brinkman as "Greendale's First Citizen, a man of high ideals and vision".

Amid all this political change, seven residents organized the Greendale Citizens Association, which pledged not to interfere in any political process, but rather to concentrate its efforts on civic improvements.

On February 25, 1939, by a vote of 238 to 110, residents approved the village manager-council form of government, effective on April 18.

Sherwood Reeder was unanimously chosen as village manager, and shortly afterward Walter Kroening was appointed assistant manager.

Since Reeder was already the village's community manager, his duties placed him in the unenvi-

MANY DIGNITARIES visited Greendale in its early years. Above is Undersecretary of Agriculture Henry Wallace (center) with Police Chief Robert Taylor (left) and George Brinkman, Greendale's first village president.

BRINKMAN FIELD was busy as the village sponsored teams in the "Big 10" suburban league. Note open area and barn to south of third base compared to today. Current Greendale residents are accustomed to a whole new view in "left field".

able position of serving both the government and the residents. In effect, it made him beholden to both landlord and tenants.

At one point, a delegation of five residents asked the executive board of the Greendale Citizens Association to demand the recall of all appointees in managerial positions in the village administration if they were being paid by the federal government. The board refused but opted to open the matter to general discussion at a citizens' meeting the following month.

Attempting to put the matter into perspective, Reeder issued a statement in which he defined the respective functions of village government and the federal manage-

READY TO SERVE, Village Manager Walter Kroening sits at his desk in the Village Hall in July of 1944 (right).

TEAM sponsored by the Greendale Theatre poses in the 1939 photo below.

ment. Briefly, he stated, the village government, as in any such community, was responsible for matters affecting the general health, welfare and protection of Greendale.

The federal government, he pointed out, was simply the landlord collecting the rents, which it doled out to the village to run its business. Therefore, he contended, the functions were not in conflict.

Besides, Reeder noted, he was elected by a unanimous vote of the Village Board to serve as village manager, despite the fact that he was the federal government's community manager at the time.

When Reeder left in 1941 for a government defense housing assignment at the naval base in San Diego, Kroening succeeded him and subsequently found himself dealing with the same dilemma.

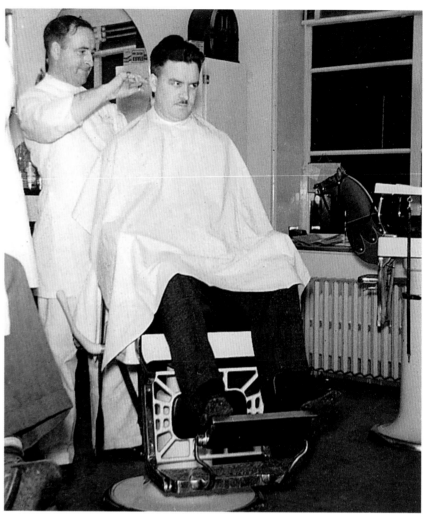

SHAVE AND A HAIRCUT was likely more than "two bits" when Archie McCosh did the clipping in 1940.

PHOTO below of Greendale's barbershop is fascinating to study. Child's horse chair was saved when the shop closed and was moved to Drews Dry Goods Store down the street.

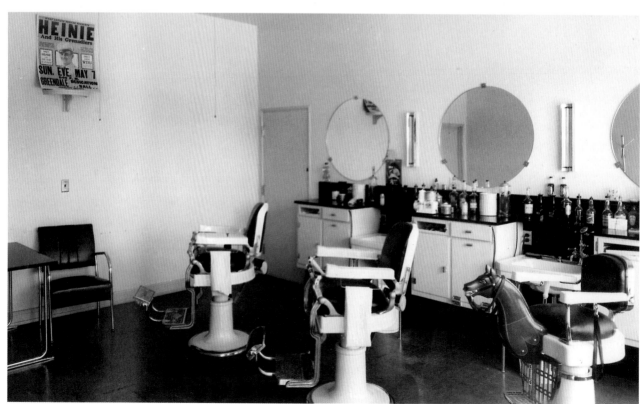

CHAPTER 18

Let the Good Times Roll

AMID ALL THESE RITES of passage as a community, Greendale's adults saw to it that good times could be had for residents of all ages. Coping with the isolating distance from Milwaukee, they organized a variety of social structures that bonded them in a unique way.

Most of the festive activities took place in the Community Building, which served as a meeting site, recreation facility and general gathering place as well as the Intermediate School (now the Middle School).

The Community Building also provided temporary worship space for church services after overflow attendances forced moves from smaller rooms in the Mercantile Building.

Activities for All

In 1938, the WPA began a recreation program in Greendale, coordinating its activities with Greendale's Recreation Committee. Jack Murdaugh's father, Charles, was named director of the government's Recreation Department for Greendale.

"He was also athletic director and a physical education teacher at the school," Jack says. "In addition, Dad helped set up and take down seats for church services in the school's multipurpose room."

The recreation organizations got social life rolling in Greendale, no doubt aided by this appeal in the *Greendale Bulletin* of August 24, 1938:

"Calling all Villagers! Calling all Villagers! Calling all Greendale talent! Do you play any in-

SWINGS were put to good use behind the Community Building, which is now Greendale's Middle School.

FORE! Greendale golfers in front of Whitnall clubhouse in 1940 are (left to right) Laverne Behning, Dorothy Reichhardt, Doris Kopisch, Rose Stefan, Jay Dobner, Rose Haag and Lydia Hartman.

struments? Can you tap dance? Are you interested in drama? Does stage-lighting or playwriting interest you?

"If you fall into any of these classifications, you may as well give yourself up now, for the Recreation Committee is seeking everywhere for all available talent."

An undated booklet recounting the early history of Greendale contained this partial rundown of events sponsored by the two recreation groups: Street dance, August 31; WPA concert, September 11; Greendale Guest Day, October 9; Hard Times Party, October 14; Children's Halloween Party, October 31; "Major Bowes" Amateur Night, November 29; Santa Claus' Visit to Greendale, December 17.

The groups organized numerous other activities, including a wom-

en's social hour to get better acquainted, while their children were being entertained in the school gym. For those inclined to tap out a beat with their feet, there was a tap danc-

"From bowling to tap dancing, there was plenty to do..."

ing class under the direction of Gretchen Kunze.

Plus there were men's and women's bowling teams...baseball teams...men's and women's gym classes...choral groups...band musicians...Boy Scout and Girl Scout troops...shop and handicrafts... dancing of all types...theatre arts... cooking classes...English and typ-

ing classes...a radio and electric group...a conservation and nature group. There was even a storytelling hour for the youngsters, hosted by Carl Fairweather—"Uncle Carl" to the children.

It wasn't long before the children had half a dozen playgrounds where they could work off their youthful energies. The Recreation Department claimed Greendale had more playgrounds per capita than any other community of comparable size.

Driving through the village today, an observer would be hard put to imagine that areas now populated by homes were once playgrounds filled with children.

There was the Apricot play center, just south of Apricot Court... the Willows playground, between Apricot and Apple Court...Basse Woods, northeast of Bluebird Court...Center Park, south of Bramble Court...Conifer, just beyond the west end of Conifer Lane...and the school playground, which was on the west side of the school building.

Many Participated

Subsequently, the Recreation Department created additional game areas: Two baseball diamonds—one on West Meadows at the west end of Northway, the other known as Athletic Field at the south end of Broad Street.

In addition, there were areas for skating rinks at Conifer and Catalpa, and at South Meadows on the east side of the village extending to Loomis Road.

Later, an area southwest of Athletic Field at Broad Street and Southway was created. "Picnic Grove" was complete with outdoor ovens for organized picnics.

Greendalers' enthusiasm for the wide range of leisure activities in their fledgling community was evident in some early statistics pulled together by the Recreation Department.

In its report of August of 1940, the department announced that total attendance at all recreational facilities for the month of July had reached 22,109. Of this total number, 18,849 was attendance at activities directly sponsored or assisted by the department.

Playground attendance totaled 11,624. The most heavily used facility was the wading pool, with an attendance of 2,276.

Speaking of baseball diamonds, Greendale experienced what may have been one of the first player strikes in baseball.

1940 Baseball Strike??

It happened in April 1940, when a group of players in the village softball league walked out of a meeting with the Recreation Department director over the amount of money allocated for the league's schedule.

Players were asked to kick in additional funds to buy the equipment. After heated discussions, a compromise was eventually worked out, and the games went on.

A WADING POOL and playground were located behind the Community Building in early 1940s. Photo below looks west of what is now the Middle School.

HORSESHOE PITS and tennis courts were near Alonzo Hauser statue in 1939. That's Broad Street on right and Village Hall is the building to the north far in the background.

SCHOOL'S OUT for the day. Driver "Woody" Wagner checks out his passengers boarding one of two school buses, which were patriotically painted red, white and blue.

CHAPTER 19

Greendale Gets Its Own School

WHILE THEIR PARENTS were preoccupied with adjusting to the newfound rigors and rewards of suburban living, the children were reveling in newfound freedoms.

Well, not completely—they still had to go to school.

School classrooms were completed in the Community Building in August 1938, and in September, 432 children became the first pupils to begin their education in Greendale. By January, enrollment was up to 525 pupils.

The school was organized into three divisions: kindergarten, elementary school (grades 1-6) and junior high school (grades 7-9). Courses were arranged to fit in with the curriculum at West Milwaukee and Pulaski, high schools on Milwaukee's south side.

John (everyone called him "Jack") R. Ambruster was named principal. For more than 20 years, he spearheaded the education of Greendale's youngsters.

His salary for that first year was $3,000. For that princely sum, he also served as superintendent and social studies teacher,

CLASSROOMS opened in the Community Building (below) in 1938. Note early model cars in front of what is now Greendale Middle School.

81

KINDERGARTEN ROOM was kept cozy with large fireplace. Teacher in foreground is Helen Ross in 1949.

plus took care of any handyman duties that needed to be done.

Ambruster came from Union Grove, where he taught future teachers at the Racine-Kenosha Normal School. Searching through hundreds of applications of those who wanted to teach in Greendale, he selected an initial staff of 20 teachers.

In one of his first actions as principal, Ambruster set up a profit-sharing store where students could buy their school supplies.

An insight into the character of the man was published in a special edition of the *Greendale Village Life* on the occasion of Greendale's 50th anniversary as a community:

"A delegator in the finest sense, Jack operated by choosing good people and letting them go to it. He and nearly all his teachers were products of the University of Chicago and its philosophy of the importance of 'social interaction in education'.

"If the kindergarten teacher wanted a little stage in her classroom so the children could 'express themselves', fine. If the music teacher wanted to pass the hat at a school concert to get money for a record player in her classroom, so be it.

"But, delegator though he was, Jack Ambruster always acted like part of the faculty, not separate from it. He also had a great sense of humor, loved a joke and took all the comedy roles in the faculty plays."

(For his dedication to the educational needs of Greendale's children

---

"The principal took all the comedy roles in the faculty plays…"

---

and to the civic good of the village, the school at South 68th Street and Greenway was later named after Ambruster. Regrettably, the school is now only a memory in his honor. Closed for 13 years, it was demolished in 2003.)

No one credited Ambruster with a great singing voice, but he enjoyed joining his teachers at Christmastime, strolling through the village and singing carols beneath the street lamps. They'd end the evening with dessert at the "Teacherage".

The "Teacherage", a description in those days of a house where teachers stayed, was the Basse farmhouse. With its 14 rooms, the farmhouse was converted into a dormitory large enough to house six or seven single teachers.

Such housing for the teachers was a necessity since there were no rooming houses, motels or hotels in Greendale or nearby. A number of teachers boarded with families.

"We had an empty bedroom because my sister had gone into the service," says Roger Klett, who was 9 years old when his family moved to Greendale in October of 1938.

"So Miss Schmidt, our civics teacher, lived with us. She stayed for two semesters, then moved into the Teacherage."

Jack Murdaugh remembers a home in the D section that housed several teachers who easily walked to work from there. "A brother of one of the teachers occupied the house and rented out rooms or just let them stay there," Jack says.

When the Teacherage had outlived its usefulness for housing, the federal government offered to lease it to Greendale's American Legion Post 416.

First Clubhouse Was in Barn

Incidentally, Post 416 was formed January 12, 1939 at a meeting of 18 service veterans in the Community Building. In November, the Legion's Ladies Auxiliary Unit held its initiation of members and installed officers.

In January of 1940, the Legion's Junior Auxiliary was organized.

The men initially held their meetings in members' homes and at the Community Building. The post later acquired its first clubhouse in a remodeled barn on Commander Lee Sowin's property.

Subsequently, members moved to temporary quarters in an abandoned construction shack at 68th and Grange. That clubhouse was later damaged by two fires, a month apart, reportedly set by vandals, children playing nearby with matches or teenagers smoking forbidden cigarettes there—depending on whose story one heard.

In any case, the blazes prompted the post to accept the government's offer of the Basse farmhouse and 3-1/2 surrounding acres in 1948.

Cost of the lease was $35 a month.

The farmhouse, then 50 years old, was sorely in need of repair. Post members immediately set about remodeling the building to suit their needs. They pitched in, many during their personal vacations, tearing down one wing of the old structure and constructing a new front for a dining room and bar.

New Watering Hole Built

Years later, the Basse farmhouse gave way to yet another Legion meeting hall, which is still on the site today. Known popularly as "Ray & Dot's", it has been the favorite watering hole for succeeding generations of Greendalers.

BASSE FARMHOUSE was first used to house teachers, then converted to a Legion Post. Note current "Ray & Dot's" Legion Building just finished behind it.

THE COMMUNITY BUILDING was pretty much the hub of Greendale during its early years. It served as a general gathering place for meetings, recreation activities and worship services before local churches were built. Photos above and below were taken during First Communion day for young members of St. Alphonsus Church.

CHAPTER 20

Village Days Celebrations Begin

NOW HOME TO more than 2,000 families, Greendale celebrated its first birthday with a 3-day round of festivities, May 5-7, 1939.

Residents and friends attended the formal dedication of the village at the Community Building on the evening of the first day. Walter Kroening opened the ceremonies with a half-hour organ recital.

Lee Sowin, president of the Greendale Citizens Association, which organized the historic event, introduced Benjamin Glassberg, a member of the Greendale Advisory Committee, who chaired the evening's ceremonies.

A veritable who's who of local and area dignitaries gave speeches, including Village Manager Sherwood Reeder; Village Board President George Brinkman; Milwaukee Mayor Daniel Hoan; Harry Muir, regional director of the Farm Security Administration; and Dr. A.T. Hatton, head of the Political Science Department at Northwestern University.

The tenor of the evening's speeches was captured in this *Milwaukee Sentinel* news story: "Feeling much as the Pilgrim fathers must have felt on the first anniversary of their settlement

FIREFIGHTER CLOWNS added fun to village's first birthday event.

on the American shore, residents of Greendale gathered at the village's community hall to hear themselves hailed as pioneers in a new era of housing as well as pioneers in bringing a return of community spirit to the urban scene."

Dr. Hatton praised Greendale's residents, saying they showed a remarkable community spirit, "something rare in cities today". He predicted, "The growth of big cities has ended and that the American culture, democracy and community spirit of the future must be nurtured in communities such as Greendale."

In closing, he remarked that he hoped to someday own a home patterned after Greendale's "honeymoon bungalows".

The Reverend Frederic Arnold, pastor of St. Alphonsus Church, gave the invocation, and the Reverend Gustav Stearns closed the evening ceremonies with a benediction.

The next day, Bob Heiss, popular announcer at Milwaukee

radio station WTMJ, broadcast his "Around the Town" talk show from the village. He interviewed the speakers of the previous evening.

Saturday and Sunday were Open House days, and hundreds of people responded to the village's invitation to visit its public buildings.

Greendale's youngsters played a role in the dedication activities, too. They participated in a tree-planting ceremony on the hill in front of the village school.

The tree was a gift from the 22 members of the first class to graduate that June from the village's Junior High School. Most of Greendale's 530 schoolchildren attended the historic planting. As the tree was lowered into the ground, representatives of each class threw shovels of dirt on its roots.

Ninth grader Harry Olson, speaking for the school, said, "We hope members of the graduating class will return in future years to see this tree."

Saturday evening, May 6, a cast of more than 150 Greendale people performed in a pageant depicting the history of the village. Written by Greendalers, it was titled "The Community of Tomorrow-Today".

The Greendale Review noted, "It would be safe to say almost every-

---

"A cast of over 150 Greendalers performed in the pageant..."

---

one in Greendale had a hand somewhere in the pageant. Their village, their lives, their hopes and joys were shown on stage."

On Sunday afternoon, Greendale's volunteer fire department competed with the Town of Lake's fire department in an exhibition of firefighting skills, climaxed by an old-fashioned water fight.

According to the *Review*, "A hilarious crowd of more than 3,000 watched the water conflict as the men of both teams were sprayed, soaked and finally dragged into the mud. But the brave lads of Greendale let nothing daunt them and went on to victory, 2-1."

At Sunday evening's dedication ball, Heinie and his Grenadiers, a popular German band heard regularly on WTMJ, performed. They provided music for dancing and entertainment by such characters as "Valter", "Villie" and "Droopy, the world's worst teller of the world's worst jokes".

Within a month of the anniversary observance, every home in Greendale had been rented, according to Roy MacAfee, tenant relations advisor.

EVERYONE got involved in the festivities, including these young boys marching down Broad Street.

GREENDALE'S FIRST FIRE DEPARTMENT was made up mostly of volunteers. Full-time or not, they all got involved in the revelry of the village's early celebrations, as evidenced by the tug-of-war on Broad Street below on the Fourth of July.

WATER GAMES were a big part of the fun during the celebration of that first anniversary of the village in 1939. In photo below, note the bleachers and trees in the open area on the east side of Broad Street. This is now the location of Dale Park.

CHAPTER 21

Social Calendars Filled Up

SOCIAL EVENTS during 1939 got off to a rousing start with a President's Ball in honor of President Franklin Roosevelt. It evolved into an annual March of Dimes Dance.

Similar events were sponsored throughout the country to raise funds to fight polio, or infantile paralysis as it was called then.

The bash was held, of course, in the auditorium of the Community Building. The event began with installation of newly elected officers of the Greendale Citizens Association, followed by refreshments and dancing to a live band.

Highlight of the evening was an auction of a huge cake—4 feet high and 9 feet in circumference—made as a replica of the nation's Capitol.

"To construct it, we baked oblong cakes in the home economics room of the school," recalls Virginia Marcus (now Fahlhaber). "I can't remember how many cakes we made. We put them all together with frosting, then made a round dome on top to represent the Capitol."

Local Boy Scouts volunteered to staff the cloakroom. Art Marcus and Warren Hale acted as masters of ceremonies.

A $100 Capitol Cake

Money was collected for refreshments, and more than $100 was generated by auctioning off portions of the cake.

After expenses, the remaining amount was donated to the national March of Dimes fund, according to a report in *The Greendale Review* of February 11.

The newspaper story also thought it appropriate to report, "Art Marcus refrained from falling into the cake long enough to auction portions."

The next year, the cake for the March of Dimes dance was baked by the Owls Club, a group of mothers of Greendale's first Boy Scouts.

The transition of the mothers from Boy Scout moms to "Owls" arose from their mutual desire to remain together after their boys got older and gave up Scouting. No longer having to raise funds and provide programs and equipment for the Scouts, the mothers continued getting together to play cards.

Art Marcus

As the story goes, they usually played past midnight before dealing the last hand and going home. Hence, someone dubbed them "Night Owls", and the moniker stuck.

It may be the same group of card players that Jack Murdaugh knew of. "There was a women's poker club that met regularly for many years," he says, discreetly neglecting to name names.

During the war, the auctions featured much sought-after items, such as silk stockings and boxes of Hershey bars, which were enthusiastically bid up and brought in good money.

Archie McCosh took over the auctioning duties for several of the succeeding dances. Police Chief Harold Bruett also held that job. By 1958, the annual cake auction was pulling in more than $400.

Greendale's momentous second year of existence, 1939, was the first time the village had a Fourth of July celebration. Attended by an estimated 1,000 people, the event in-

CAPITOL CAKE from 1942 dance (above) is being cut by Helen Stark, Mrs. Len Underdale and Mrs. E. Zillmer.

PICNICS and outings were popular in 1945. That's Al Hanel facing camera while working at church booth below.

> ## *"The women's group was called 'Night Owls' because they played cards past midnight..."*

cluded games...a children's parade with prizes for the most original decorations...contests for the grown-ups...community singing... and a basket picnic in the school woods at Broad Street and Southway.

There was also a fat man's race. Any male weighing more than 200 pounds was eligible. Obesity led to ingenuity for lack of a better reason, and the participants decided to form a club. The heavyweights called themselves the Hippo Club.

Not long afterward, the Greendale Men's Club (dues were 25¢ a month) came into existence at a get-together of a village baseball group at Al Washkowiak's home on Azalea Court.

The spirit of the time was captured in this news item in the *Greendale Bulletin*: "Jot Wednesday night, August 31, 7:30 p.m., in your little date book and get ready for a really old-fashioned, enjoyable fun fest in the Greendale style and spirit.

"Don't forget to drag those dancing shoes out of the mothballs, for

MARCH OF DIMES DANCE in 1942 was a fund-raiser to help fight polio. That looks like the "Grand March" above.

GOOD-LOOKING BUNCH below are (left to right) Shirley Weber, Art Niemczyk, and Charlie and Mardelle Humpal.

there's going to be a big, free street dance on Broad Street for all residents. Music will be furnished by a nine-piece swing band with rhythm that just tickles the toes. The entertainment will include a marionette show for the kiddies and other types of amateur performances."

Rounding out the social calendar that year was a Guest Day in October and the Christmas Frolic.

4,000 Visitors Came to Look

Guest Day provided residents with an opportunity to show off their new digs to visitors—not that they hadn't had a lot of people dropping in on them already. They served as hosts and hostesses to an estimated *4,000 visitors* that day, treating them to tours of homes and various public facilities.

Local talent, under Charles Murdaugh's direction, offered a continuous round of entertainment in the Community Building auditorium. Recreation Department staffers provided playground activities for the children of visiting parents.

JULY FOURTH PARADES have always been popular in Greendale. At left, 1945.

WINNERS of "Tin Can Alley" contest in 1943 (below) are Bob Sullivan, Bill Sullivan, Gene Mund and Ron Underdale.

CHAPTER 22

Recreational Facilities Are Built

ALONG WITH their newfound neighborhood friends, Greendale families soon discovered such local delights as ice skating and Skunk Hollow.

"Ice skating was one of the big activities in wintertime," recalls Jack Murdaugh. "I remember skating on the tennis courts right in front of the Intermediate School. There was a small shack there with a potbellied stove.

"The courts were often flooded at night so they'd freeze enough for us to skate on them the next day. My dad would go out at midnight and add water. Everybody just helped out."

The tennis courts, incidentally, also served as an open-air dance floor during those early summers. Upwards of 400 to 500 people would trip the light fantas-

SKATING RINK at end of Clover Lane kept Greendale kids busy in winter. Photo below is from January 1944.

COMMUNITY SANDBOX was popular at Willow Park (now Pioneer Park).

tic outdoors to the music of local Big Bands.

"The ballpark, now Brinkman Field, was also flooded in the winter," Jack continues.

"We skated at other places in the area. One was on the pond by the clubhouse in Whitnall Park. There was an island out there, and it was fun to skate around the island. We used to skate on some of the quarries in the area, too. Ice skating was popular, cheap and a lot of fun."

Karen Fogelberg's favorite ice skating rink was the one on Clover Lane, where the Greendale Community Church now stands.

"The best part about skating there was the warming house," she says. "They always had a nice fire going, and we kids could sit in there and have a lot of fun just talking."

John Miller sheds some light on the origin of that warming house. It was a Quonset hut at Whitnall Park that had housed Civilian Conservation Corps workers.

"It was eventually moved to Scout Lake and became known as the Scout Shack for Troop 505," John recounts. "As Boy Scouts, we spent a lot of time there."

"The Scout Shack in those days was only half of what it is today," adds Jack Murdaugh. "It had a stage, wooden benches and a woodstove. I enjoyed smelling the wood burning, and feeling nice and cozy inside during our Scout meetings in winter, then walking home through the woods in the dark on a cold night."

Scout Shack Kept Moving

The Milwaukee County Park Commission wanted the building moved from Scout Lake, and in 1949 donated it to Troop 505, which obtained permission from the school board to relocate it to a semi-wooded area of the elementary school grounds at the foot of Crocus Court, where it still stands today.

To move the large building, the dining hall was sawed in half, then the halves were moved separately and reassembled at the new site.

As Scouting use of the building grew over the next 9 years, it became apparent the structure needed to be expanded. Under the leadership of the Reverend Maurice Terry, then chairman of Troop 505, a Youth Memorial Building Committee was formed to plan the expansion and raise the necessary funds.

One such group helping to preserve the building was the Greendale Minstrels, a male group created in 1939 primarily to raise money for various community causes. The group performed a special show with all funds going for the building, and the event was well attended.

A year of campaigning yielded less than the $10,000 goal. But with a combination of some $7,000 in cash, donated materials and volunteer labor, the expansion was finally accomplished.

The expanded Youth Memorial Building was formally dedicated on October 4, 1967. Over the years, remodeling and additions have been made to the structure for use by various organizations. Its future is un-

YOUTH MEMORIAL BUILDING was first located at Scout Lake. It had to be sawed in half to accommodate its move to its present location near Crocus Court.

certain. The School District may tear it down to create space for additional school facilities.

Skunk Hollow Was Popular

A favorite playground with an unlikely name, "Skunk Hollow" was located in a dirt and grass valley of woods between the water tower west of Conifer Lane, near the Crocus Court apartments.

"That's where everybody went," says Vicki Glynn, whose family was one of the first Greendale tenants. "I don't know why we called it Skunk Hollow. I think it was because skunk cabbage was once raised in the area."

"Not too many kids would go sledding there," recalls John Miller. "There was one bad bump that made it a terrible jump among the rocks and trees."

Karen Fogelberg loved Skunk Hollow in the summer. "We'd go there early in the morning and pick the most beautiful wild raspberries. Then Mom would make a pie that was out of this world!"

Boys Did Daring Stunts

She also participated in a more daring adventure at Skunk Hollow. "A couple of us were there snapping pictures for our photography class at school," Karen recounts. "We saw a couple of the older boys on top of the water tower, and one guy was hanging off the side railing by his hands! I got a picture of that. I could have blackmailed him, but he's still one of my best friends."

Dick Lenten doesn't confess to being the kid doing the stunt, but he admits being there.

"I didn't have that much nerve," he says. "I just walked around the railing, which was pretty scary in itself up there. In fact," he elaborates, "there was more than one guy doing a handstand on the railing."

Dick also recalls the time some-

WATER TOWER was like a magnet to boys who got in trouble climbing it.

95

LARGE LONE ELM TREE on east side of Broad Street was a popular gathering spot. There were no buildings on east side of street until 1958.

one spray-painted "Hi, Old Mary Field" on the water tower. "She was the assistant principal at the high school at the time, and I didn't do it!" he insists.

The water tower was an irresistible attraction to John Miller, too. "We climbed it a lot because it was available, and there was no fence around it," he surmises. "We'd often climb to the very top of the tank, then slide down a bit to a trapdoor, where we could look inside the tower and see water.

"One day we spotted a policeman coming out of the woods. It was Chief Bruett. We tried to get down fast, but he got to the tower before we could scramble down. He took us to the police station, where we got a good talking-to," John recalls ruefully. "He scared us enough to keep us off the water tower for a month or two."

A safer attraction was a large elm tree on the east side of Broad Street. It stood at the north end of an open field known as Central Park. There were no stores on that side of the street then.

"Everybody would gather there,

especially for the Fourth of July," remembers Evelyn Truppe.

"It was a nice open space for the kids. I was afraid of a huge black crow that made its home in the tree. Whenever I went there, he'd go after me the minute he saw me."

"A lot of us learned to play sheepshead underneath that tree," adds John Miller. ("Sheepshead", for those who have never been dealt

---

"There was more than one guy doing a handstand on the water tower railing..."

---

a hand in this mysterious and wonderful card game, is perhaps known only to Milwaukeeans. It resembles no other card game, except maybe pinochle, with its assortment of "trumps" and limited number of cards.)

Karen Fogelberg describes a more refined good time under that tree. "One of my favorite things to do in summer was to sit under the

tree with a good book from the library, a bag of potato chips and a Hershey bar," she says. "I'd read and listen to the bugs buzzing around, and look up at the sky and think how wonderful life was."

"We all hung out there," adds Diane Robbins. "I remember we'd build bonfires near the tree. There was also a bandstand nearby."

The bandstand, according to some reports, was nothing more than a wooden platform.

"About a half dozen musicians, led by Al Hall, played evenings there when the weather was nice," recalls Jim Kendellen. "That tree was a landmark."

Unfortunately, it was sacrificed for Greendale's future the day that side of the street gave way to a row of stores (see more in Chapter 39).

"I was so angry the day they cut it down. I didn't even want to go and watch," says Evelyn. "But I guess it had to be done."

CHAPTER 23

'Aunt Jen' Kept Kids Busy

DICK LENTEN recalls the good old days at Central Park (now Dale Park), just east of Broad Street, which was near his house. "We played lots of baseball there," he says.

There was no need for Greendale youngsters to "just hang out", due to endless activities being offered. As recreation director, Jennie Butler gave them lots of choices.

It was more than a job to "Aunt Jen", as this tiny lady was affectionately called by the teenagers she supervised. A widow, she adopted Greendale's children as her own.

She Was a "Second Mom"

"The children loved Jennie because she first loved them," local freelance writer Doris Krupinski recalled some years ago in her popular, long-running "View from the Hill" column in the *Greendale Village Life* newspaper.

"Jennie was like the mother to us all," Karen Fogelberg recalls lovingly. "She was a very sweet lady, always there for us."

JENNIE BUTLER, recreation director, treated all children like her own.

"Jennie was really a friend to everybody," Carla (Reichhardt) Cabanatuan echoes.

As recreation director, Jennie started out pretty much on her own. She managed without funds and equipment, making do with donations and whatever equipment she could locate.

Doris Krupinski recalls one source of Jennie's funds: "She found a pool table somewhere, and by charging 15¢ a game, she had enough money to buy supplies and keep the equipment in repair.

Jennie Got Things Done

"Using the $50 she accumulated from the pool table charge, she replaced an old 78-rpm phonograph in the teen center with a new 45-rpm record player."

Jennie first set up a recreational facility in the CCC building that

LOCALS LOVED IT when Wisconsin Governor Oscar Rennebohm made sodas at Casey's Grill in 1948.

remained from the construction of the village, then later moved the center into the basement of the school. It was open evenings and after school.

There she held dances for the teenagers, organized summertime playground activities, set up arts and crafts programs for the small children during the summer, recruited volunteers to give drama lessons and did whatever else would make the center a magnet for her children.

"I remember the jukebox dances there on Fridays," says Vicki Glynn. "Afterward, everybody would go to Casey's Grill on Broad Street for hamburgers and Cokes."

Gathered at Soda Fountain

With the opening of the village's first drugstore in the Mercantile Building, complete with an old-time soda fountain, another venue of fun opened up for Greendale's young people.

The drugstore, the first privately operated business enterprise in the village, was subleased from the Co-op by Kendall Des Jardin, who had previously managed a pharmacy on Milwaukee's east side.

It opened for business on April 15, 1939 and received a banner reception. More than 1,000 persons

> **"Over 1,000 people visited the drugstore on its first day…"**

visited the drugstore that first day, eating in its grillroom and sampling the goodies at the soda fountain.

"I estimated we served 500 people at the soda fountain alone," recalls Ken. Equally busy that inaugural day was Ken's wife, Jeanette, who was in charge of the grillroom.

Indeed, it proved to be a busy first year. "I worked 7 days a week for 1 solid year," Ken recalls. "Neither one of us took a day off. I was in the store from 8:30 in the morning till 11 at night."

Jeanette, too, remembers her hectic schedule, balancing the care of their boy, Ken Jr., with her grillroom duties.

"At 11 a.m., I'd put Ken in the buggy, take him to the drugstore and put him in the back room," she says. "If he started crying, I'd bring him into the kitchen, where he could see me. At 2, I'd take him home, give him his lunch, put him down for his nap and do the laundry.

"Later, I'd get supper ready. At 7 o'clock, our baby-sitter would come in, and I'd take Ken's meal to him at the store, where we'd both work until 11."

"We didn't take time off because we had borrowed money from suppliers and from Jeanette's father," Ken says. "We worked until we got all the bills paid. But, it wasn't anything that anyone couldn't do."

The couple was lenient with customers who couldn't always pay their bills. "We gave people credit whenever they needed it, and I kept track in a little book," Ken says. "In all our years in Greendale, I lost only $10 in a bad check. That's all."

One fellow Greendaler owed them a fair amount of money. "He had emphysema real bad," recalls Ken. "The family didn't have any money, and his wife and kids all worked to help pay his hospital bill. Then his father died and left him a little land, which he sold. The first person he paid was me. He came in and paid up his bill."

There were times Ken's workday didn't end at 11 p.m., like the night the doctor called about 2 a.m. saying he was delivering a baby and needed ether.

"He knew where I lived and said he'd be right over to drive me to the store. I pulled on a pair of pants but didn't have time to slip into shoes before he arrived. Before I could get

FIRST DRUGSTORE was run by Kendall Des Jardin, holding Kendall Jr., and wife Jeanette. Above, they're in front of the store in 1941. Below is inside view of store when it first opened in '39.

into the car, he took off like a bat. I stood on the running board all the way to the store.

"I went in, got the ether, came out and gave it to the doctor," Ken continues. "He said, 'Thanks a lot' and drove away, leaving me standing there in my bare feet. I walked home like that."

It wasn't long before the soda fountain became a favorite gathering place. "The kids would come there at noon and have a little lunch," he says. "They'd come back after school and get a Coke. Then about 4 o'clock, I'd say, 'Okay, it's time to go home,' and they would all go.

"The kids weren't allowed to roam around the store proper, and if I caught somebody doing that, I just said, 'Do you want me to tell your folks or should I talk to Father Spangler (the pastor at St. Alphonsus)?' That did it."

"The kids really couldn't get away with too much, because Ken knew all their parents," Jeanette adds. "We weren't a big-city type of town. We were a small town, and we had fun."

SODA FOUNTAIN in the drugstore was a popular gathering place for kids at lunchtime and after school.

BUSY GUY. Kendall Des Jardin (below) recalls being at drugstore from 8:30 a.m. to 11 p.m., 7 days a week.

CHAPTER 24

Theatre Opens on Broad Street

TWO WEEKS after the drugstore's grand opening, there was lots of excitement and anticipation in the village. The magic of Hollywood came to town with the opening of the Greendale Theatre.

Continuing its policy of subleasing certain businesses to private individuals, the Co-op's board of directors chose Erwin Koenigsreiter to manage it. Erwin was a veteran in the theatre business, starting as an usher when he was 16, and had managed most of downtown Milwaukee's first-run movie houses.

The theatre, which seated 650, opened on Saturday, April 29, 1939 with a single feature, *Out West with the Hardys*, starring the irrepressible Mickey Rooney as Andy Hardy. According to the ad in *The Greendale Review*, the gala opening program also presented "selected short subjects and the latest news events for real family entertainment".

Double Features Popular

The turnout was wonderful, reported Koenigsreiter, who said, "I'm especially pleased at the interest and pride the villagers have shown in their new theatre."

Along with this glowing account, *The Greendale Review* reported results of a survey by the theatre, in which patrons said they favored double features over single ones.

Shortly afterward, patrons got their wish and got to sit through such movie pairings as *Dawn Patrol*, starring Errol Flynn, with *Four Girls in White*, starring Kent

"Harvey would take a pair of scissors and cut a guy's tie off…"

Taylor; *Alexander's Ragtime Band* with *Nancy Drew, Reporter*; and *There Goes My Heart*, featuring Fredric March and Virginia Bruce, with *Mr. Moto's Last Warning*, starring Peter Lorre.

To help stimulate continued interest in the theatre, *The Greendale Review* began publishing the names of 10 residents chosen at random, hiding their names throughout each issue. The lucky finders received two free theatre passes if they claimed them at

the theatre before the next issue.

Koenigsreiter next introduced "dish night", joining the latest craze sweeping the country. The Great Depression had drained family incomes, and people were shelling out fewer and fewer hard-earned dimes and quarters for a night out at the movies.

But the promise of receiving free cups, saucers, plates, platters, gravy bowls and the rest—one item for each night's attendance until a complete dinnerware set was accumulated—lured people back to the theatre in Greendale as well.

The free dinnerware was handed out to the village ladies on Thursday and Friday nights for the price of a regular admission ticket. "I think my mom still has some of those dishes in her attic," says Bill Henrichs.

Variety Store Opens

In July of 1939, the village's first very own department store opened. It was known back then as "a dry goods and variety store".

Located in the Mercantile Building, the store was leased by the Frank Specialty Company, a Milwaukee wholesaler. Harvey

GREENDALE THEATRE opened in 1939. Now site of Great Harvest Bread Co., theatre aspects are still visible inside.

PANORAMIC VIEW of west Broad Street (below) shows vintage cars, milk truck and tall smokestack of heating plant.

① Supermarket ② Variety Store ③ Drug Store

④　　⑤　　⑥　　⑦　　⑧　　⑨　　　　　　⑩　　　　　　　　　⑪

ooking West of Entire Shopping Center(exclusive of Garage)
Greendale, Wis.

⑤ Bank ⑥ Shoe Shop ⑦ Barber Shop ⑧ Grill ⑨ Appliances ⑩ Post Office & Drs. Offices ⑪ Tavern.

Wegner was the first manager.

The store promised "a selection of the very latest style goods available". That included ladies and men's sportswear, dresses, lingerie, towels and washcloths, household items and hardware, school supplies, toiletries, greeting cards and much more.

Store Was "Friendly Place"

Opening day was hailed as a "colossal success", according to Manager Wegner. "Almost everyone who entered the store was able to find the particular item desired. In a few cases we had to order items not stocked. However, as soon as we learn what customers want, we will make every effort to secure those articles."

Emilie Cywinski, one of the first residents living on Dendron Lane, worked as a clerk at the variety store after graduating from high school.

"It was a very friendly place," she recalls. "Ida Crandall and Alice Voight worked with me, and we got along fine and enjoyed meeting the people. We weren't overworked. We worked 6 days a week, 8 hours a day."

Wegner was a practical joker, according to Ken Des Jardin.

"Harvey and the other businessmen in the village would come to the drugstore for lunch," Ken recounts. "Harvey would take out a pair of scissors, reach over and cut a guy's tie off. Then he'd take him over to the store and give him a new one."

Wegner's pioneer association with the store and with Greendale ended 6 years later. The store's lease expired in May of 1945, and the Greendale Co-operative Association took over operation of the store.

CHRISTMAS PARTY at village's Variety Store hosted by Manager Harvey Wegner drew a big crowd, especially with Santa on hand.

Early Greendale merchants came up with all sorts of promotions to lure customers, but likely there wasn't a better promoter than theatre manager Erwin Koenigsreiter. "Dish Night" was one of his best—each person got a free plate, saucer, etc. each time they attended—and they had to keep coming to complete the set!

The Greendale Review worked with Koenigsreiter to promote readership and the movies—they hid names of 10 residents in each issue, and finders got two free theatre passes. Clever!

CHAPTER 25

There's a Tavern in the Town

THE SAME MONTH the department store opened—July of 1939—the village's first and only tavern swung open its doors at the corner of Northway and Broad Street.

The lease for the Greendale Tavern was awarded to Fred Staub, whose experience included more than a decade of operating and working in restaurants and taverns in Milwaukee.

Hastening to reassure any residents who might be less than enthusiastic about the village's new social venture, Staub was quoted in *The Greendale Review* as saying, "I wish to give Greendale and the surrounding area a clean, orderly place of diversion.

"I want to give good service and conduct my place of business so that it will be a social center in the old-fashioned way, a place where visitors may come in for something to eat and drink,

GREENDALE TAVERN, in 1939, is now Heinemann's Restaurant. Note flat-topped post office next door.

THE BAR at Village Inn offered fish fries for 35¢ in 1948. Jack Blosser, shown here, was manager then.

and then stay to chat with their neighbors."

"A lot of people went to the tavern for fish fries on Friday nights," states Jack Murdaugh. "But our family didn't do that very often because my dad, being a teacher, felt he had to be a little careful about where he was seen."

Other residents evidently took Fred Staub at his word. *The Greendale Review* reported, "Hundreds were served with food and drinks on the opening day, and the enthusiasm has not waned.

"The first customer was Fabian Strong, who slapped down five pennies on the counter and ordered the first glass of beer."

Within a year, the tavern changed management, with the nod going to Joe Sullivan, who lived right across the street on Municipal Square. With the departure of Fred Staub, the Co-op Board considered operating the tavern as a Co-op enterprise.

But a special committee appointed by the board concluded that until loans on the other Co-op enter-

prises were paid, no money was available for such a venture. Accordingly, the tavern was again subleased, this time to Sullivan, who promptly renamed the establishment the Greendale Village Inn.

Joe's son, Bob, who was 10 years old at the time, remembers his dad as "a very outgoing and popular guy. He was entrepreneurial and seemed to be working all the time.

"My mother ran the kitchen at the tavern, and they would have lunch-

---

"The Friday night fish fry dinners were 35¢ each..."

---

es every day for the people who worked the night shifts at Allis-Chalmers and other places in Milwaukee," Bob recalls. "She also served the fish fries on Friday nights. They were 35¢."

Bob helped out by going to the tavern every few days to fill up the back bar with bottles of beer. "They didn't have all those rules and regu-

lations that they do now," Bob adds.

The following month, the Greendale Beauty Salon, managed by Helen Huebner, held an open house to announce its presence in the village.

To entice Greendale housewives into the shop, "equipped with all the latest equipment for permanent waving and all other branches of beauty culture," specials and souvenirs were offered. "A beautiful Juva Tex automatic compact will be given with any permanent, and smaller gifts for other services," the promotion stated.

A small radio repair store also opened on the street, operated by Bramble Burke in addition to his full-time job as a telephone employee in Milwaukee.

The double workload convinced him to give up the store. Subsequently, Tom Hartman took over and built the business into a full-service store offering appliances and TV

RURAL ASPECT of early Greendale is obvious in the photo above taken in 1939 of house at 5714 Clover Lane.

HIGH SCHOOL STUDENTS (below) took part in a civic project by helping in village grocery store in 1948.

and radio repair work.

Amid all the "firsts" during that summer of 1939, Greendale recorded its first two marriages on the same day, July 1. Harry Brandt, of Angle Lane, and Caroline Clausing, of Grange Place, said their vows at the Community Building in a ceremony conducted by the Reverend Mohrhoff, pastor of St. Luke's.

"Wally and I were part of the group that 'shivareed' them," says Evelyn Truppe.

The Brandt newlyweds missed, by 18 months, being married in the white wooden structure that was constructed to serve as St. Luke's Church.

In the second marriage that day, Carl Berliner and Catherine Cain, both of Milwaukee, traveled to Greendale to say their vows before Justice of the Peace Henry Radtke in the home of Clem Donnelly.

On another social note of historical significance, Greendale's first set of twins, Larry and Gary, were born to Mr. and Mrs. Ronald Danielson, of Arbutus Court, in August of '39.

ST. LUKE'S LUTHERAN CHURCH on Northway (below) was a white wooden structure in 1941. It was 18 months from being completed when Harry Brandt and Caroline Clausing (left) were married on July 1,1939. So they were married in the Community Building. Theirs was the first marriage in the village, followed closely by a second marriage that same day—Carl Berliner and Catherine Cain, who said their vows in the home of Clem Donnelly.

CHAPTER 26

New Library in Big Demand

IN OCTOBER of 1940, a library was set up in the north wing of the Community Building to serve both the residents and the village school.

Apparently Greendalers were itching to borrow those library books, to the point that an appeal was published in the *Greendale Bulletin*, asking that villagers stop inquiring when the library will be opened:

"It seems desirable to state at this time that the work in the library will be greatly facilitated if the villagers will wait until the date for the formal opening is announced through the pages of this bulletin.

"The two librarians and their assistants have been working steadily to get the books organized."

89 Books Out First Hour

When the library opened on October 17, it initially offered 2,379 volumes of children's and adults' books, plus a "well-selected list of magazines for general reading".

Eighty-nine books were taken

out in the first hour, between 3 and 4 p.m. And 295 residents applied for "borrower" cards during the first 3 days.

The honor of receiving the first library card went to 14-year-old Pat Moran. She later married to Earl Goetsch, and they lived on

Bramble Court. Pat's family had moved into Greendale just in time for her to join the first ninth-grade class in the village's school in the Community Building.

Teenagers graduating from ninth grade in Greendale's school system had to switch to either

YOUNG AND OLD eagerly awaited the library set up in Community Building.

BOY SCOUT BAND posed for this picture in front of the library entrance to Community Building. Troop 505 started in 1939.

READING provided inexpensive entertainment for early residents (below), who spent a good deal of time in the library.

Time to Repaint All Houses

WHEN Walter Kroening became village manager in 1941, one of his first actions was to order repainting of the exteriors and interiors of Greendale's homes. This was generally popular and became a major topic of conversation among residents.

Kroening stated the exteriors would be painted in varying shades of buff and white, and the interiors a cream buff. Those colors, he said, were chosen by a color consultant, Captain Ledyard Towle, who was called in to assist management in the project.

Captain Towle was described as a "camouflage expert", since he had recently acted as consultant to British military officials. (He reportedly later designed colors for many of Detroit's automobiles.)

Somehow, though, Captain Towle's opinions on color were brushed aside. Questionnaires were distributed to housewives, asking them to state their interior color preferences.

Some 200 women cast ballots for their favorite colors. Kroening announced that the eight most preferred colors would be stocked, from which the housewives could choose when it came time to paint rooms in their homes.

"A few simple rules," Kroening said, "will apply to their use: The same color, preferably with a high light reflection value, is to be chosen for the living room and stair hall. Individual colors may be used in the bedrooms.

"Powder blue will only be permitted in bedrooms having more than one exposure because of its low light reflection value. Ivory or buff may be used for ceilings. No change is contemplated in the type or color of enamel now used in kitchens and baths."

Kroening estimated the village face-lift would cost about $94,000 and consume some 10,000 gallons of paint. No records are available to determine how close he came with his estimate. The buff and white exteriors remain on many of the homes to this day.

THEY PAINTED THE TOWN. Well, the original homes, at least, both inside and out, in 1941. The group pictured below brushed on an estimated *10,000 gallons* of paint. They deserved a picnic afterward.

Pulaski or West Milwaukee high school to complete their education. Sometimes they carpooled; often they hitchhiked.

"I did a lot of hitchhiking," responds Jim Curtin, whose father was one of the first doctors to set up a practice in Greendale. "Most of the time, we'd get rides from people who'd drop us off right at the school.

"I never got to use my dad's car because he had to have it at all times, in case he had to make a house call," Jim says. "But I didn't resent not having a car. That's the way it was back then. I accepted it; it had to be.

"What was rougher was telling a Milwaukee kid you were from Greendale," Jim recalls. "They'd laugh their heads off and say,

'You're a hick. What are you doing way out in the sticks?'

"Most people thought we weren't as good as they were. They got that idea mostly from the local newspaper, which always wrote us up as to the kind of town this was—well, government housing, and all that."

Diane Robbins, who had just entered a high school in Milwaukee,

"DREAM HOUSE" like one at left was offered as the prize in a contest to raise funds for Youth Memorial Building in the village. Jacquelyn Robbins' jingle (below) won the house. Above is another example of bending streets.

wasn't happy at first about coming "way out to Greendale".

"I was at that age when kids hate to move. All my friends were back there. Here, I had no friends," she recalls wistfully. "But it wasn't long before I realized what a beautiful little community we'd come to."

Won a Dream House

Despite Diane's initial misgivings, her parents moved to Greendale because her mother, Jacquelyn, had won a "Dream House" on Cornflower Lane in a jingle contest. The house was advertised as being worth $10,000, and an entry blank cost just 50¢.

Funds from the contest were to be earmarked for the Youth Memorial Building in the village, which would serve as a combined Legion Hall and Community Center.

Sponsored by Greendale's American Legion Post 416, the contest attracted entries from all over the na-

> ### *"They'd laugh their heads off when they heard we were from Greendale..."*

tion, even from Guam and Vienna, despite the contest's lagging sales in the beginning. After about 3 months

of selling the 50-cent entry blanks, the post had accumulated only about $1,300 to offset the $8,100 that local Legion officials estimated the post had spent on the house.

"We tried everything—radio, newspaper advertising, letters to all Legion posts in the state, posters and ticket distribution, but it didn't work," says William Burke, the post's finance officer.

They decided to extend the contest beyond the September 7th entry deadline. Sales never did reach a profitable level. Finally, the contest was ended with an announcement of the winner at an Armistice Day Ball in the Community Building.

Diane can still recite her mother's winning jingle:

> *"Oh give me a home,*
> *a home of my own,*
> *with room for a*
> *youngster or two.*
> *So sings my wife,*
> *the light of my life,*
> *since our landlord says*
> *tots are taboo."*

And that's how the Robbins family and their two youngsters came to live in Greendale.

IN THE SERVICE OF OUR COUNTRY

CHAPTER 27

Rationing a Wartime Sacrifice

WORLD WAR II left its imprint on Greendale like any other community. On the home front, residents struggled with the uncertainties of the times, made sacrifices and dealt with wartime restrictions.

Prompted by patriotic fervor, as much as those restrictions, Greendalers held one of the nation's first aluminum drives in June of 1941.

An enclosure was set up in front of the Village Hall to receive light metal, a vital component of warplanes. A slogan, "From Pots and Pans to Planes", was coined to encourage participation.

"The pile of aluminum stacked up in front of the Village Hall was pretty big," Dick Lenten recalls. "Everyone got together and pitched in."

To determine if Greendale housewives would part with their pots and pans, Village Manager Walter Kroening asked six families to check their kitchen shelves and see how many of their aluminum utensils they would be willing to part with.

"Most of the housewives told me they had aluminum house
wares they rarely or never used, but that they hesitated to throw them away," he commented.

The village's households con-

WWII HONOR ROLL was posted in front of the post office building, which still stands behind "Eleanor's Fountain".

IN THE SERVICE OF OUR COUNTRY

113

tributed more than 1,000 pots and pans, amounting to 370 pounds of aluminum, plus another 135 pounds of copper and brass. The contributions included bottle caps and two washing machines—one donated by Rae Getter of Apricot Court, then assistant editor of *The Greendale Review*.

Youngsters were active in the drive, too. Children donated old toys, from play dishes to worn-out metal coaster wagons, and the Boy Scouts went from house to house, collecting the discards.

Roger Klett was one of those youngsters. "We all participated, scrounging around the neighborhood looking for aluminum. We got a lot of it from a dump where the water tower is now," he says.

The 6-day haul was sold to a Milwaukee smeltery for 11-1/2¢ a pound for the aluminum, and 8¢ a pound for the copper and brass. The money, slightly more than $50, went to the Greendale Defense Council, formed as a further community contribution to the war effort.

Greendale's home front war effort asserted itself again in a paper drive that July. The first week's collection yielded 3-1/2 tons of paper and over 500 pounds of rags. And again, Boy Scout Troop 505 was in the vanguard of the drive. Tugging their coasters around the village, the

---

"Greendalers held one of the nation's first aluminum drives..."

Scouts collected 9,375 pounds of wastepaper in December, a 1-month record.

Subsequently, the collection of wastepaper, scrap metal and various sundries settled into a major organizational community effort. Boxes placed at the Co-op Market, Des Jardins' Drugstore and the Village Inn were for cigarette tinfoil and toothpaste tubes. Scrap metal went into a container at the Co-op Gas Station.

The Cub Scouts picked up the

WORLD WAR II RATION BOARD poses in 1940. They first set up office in one of the originals on Clover Lane.

boxes, and village servicemen kept an eye out for the scrap metal. Housewives were encouraged to save rubber materials, tin cans, old lightbulbs and outdated license plates.

The tin cans, residents were reminded, must be flattened to obtain the lowest freight shipping rate. They were instructed to not use a hammer to flatten the cans, but to stomp on them, just as they would "on a cockroach".

The drive to save everything reached scrupulous levels. Anyone buying toothpaste or shaving cream at the drugstore had to turn in a used tube, or it was "no sale".

Erv Koenigsreiter held a "Victory Show" at his theatre—village youngsters were admitted for the price of five old keys. That netted some 25 to 30 pounds of keys, which would later be used to make bullets.

"The line of youngsters waiting to get in reached far down Broad Street," reported *The Greendale Review*. For their keys, the young people saw a Jane Withers movie, a deep-sea feature and several comedies.

In addition, residents responded to exhortations to buy defense stamps and bonds. Although money was in short supply, they bought nearly $200 worth of stamps and some $250 in bonds during the weekend following Pearl Harbor.

A loudspeaker system, mounted in the Village Hall and on street corners, blanketed the village with patriotic messages and music, urging purchases. In total, Greendale sponsored eight war bond drives.

Sugar Rationing Snafu

During the war, almost everything on civilian consumer shelves was rationed.

Carol Curtin was a member of the ration board for the village. "We had to decide if people qualified for ration books, gasoline, fuel oil and tires," she explains. "We were also in charge of price controls, and we checked taverns and restaurants to keep their prices in line.

"Our first office was in an original Greendale house at the south end of Clover Lane," Carol says. "Ella Miller was the chief clerk, and the kitchen was her private office. Grace Lange and I sat at desks facing each other in the dinette. In the living room was a long table where people filled out their applications for rations," Carol recalls.

"Being a government agency, we weren't allowed to accept gratuities, but occasionally around Christmas, when we'd leave the office, we would find a bottle of Scotch at the doorstep."

(Near the end of the war, the ration board set up shop in larger offices in the former beauty shop quarters on Broad Street.)

Pioneer families recall the local sugar rationing snafu of 1942. It wasn't until some 900 sugar ration books had been handed out to village families on April 24 that John Ambruster, local rationing administrator, was informed the distribution was premature.

State rationing officials had intended the distribution that day to be only a " test run" for the actual national handout starting on May 4.

Ambruster was now faced with the need to retrieve the books, because, as *The Greendale Review* story put it, "The principle objection (to the premature distribution) was the fact that villagers who received their books on Friday could go out and purchase as much sugar as they wanted before the sugar freeze order became effective the following Monday, April 27."

No fear of that, apparently: "County officials replied they expected Greendalers to be patriotic enough to refrain from such a practice."

Ambruster immediately sent his workers out around the village, knocking on doors and gathering up the errant ration books. And no-

A CIVIL DEFENSE SETUP in advance of a drill was put in place in the gym of the Community Building. Shown is Walter Kroening, village manager, with Merrill Burke and Cecelia Hensley.

tices were distributed throughout the community.

Whether all the books were recaptured isn't known exactly, only that "workers reported uniformly courteous receptions from the somewhat bewildered citizenry," noted *The Greendale Review*.

Eleanor Jolly remembers the hardships of gas rationing. "We had our first nice car about then," she said, "but we didn't get to enjoy driving it a lot because we were allowed only 5 gallons of gas a week.

"Al took the bus back and forth to his job as a night pressroom foreman at *The Milwaukee Journal*. It wasn't easy for him. We ended up selling the car for about the same price we paid for it."

Judy Birch recalls getting in line for her milk and sugar. "Being a very early riser, I was usually the

first one there before the ration office opened," she says. "It's a good thing I did because the line was always very long."

Drugstore operator Ken Des Jardin remembers his problems with wartime rationing. "We had trouble

getting merchandise, especially baby food," he says. "And with all the babies in Greendale, I couldn't get enough. I used to drive to Milwaukee and stop at every drugstore and pick up what I could. We couldn't be without that."

COLLECTIONS of all sorts were common during the early '40s. Lee Spratter (far right) supervises a paper drive.

CUB SCOUTS march north on Broad Street in 1940. Note the Co-op store, and "Greendale statue" in background.

CHAPTER 28

Greendale Men Head Off to War

THE Greendale Defense Council, in one of its first tasks, assisted Milwaukee Selective Service Board No. 29 in registering young men for the national draft.

Some 30 women and two men volunteered to serve on the draft board. They helped register Greendale men, ages 20 through 44, on February 15, 1942 in the Village Hall. Juanita May was in charge of the sign-ups that day.

Joining the armed forces and leaving home—many for the first time in their lives—was bound to bring on homesickness. Greendale Defense Council members did their bit to keep up the morale of service personnel.

On a Sunday afternoon and evening in June of 1942, the council hosted a huge hospitality party that drew some 200 servicemen from homes in all parts of the nation.

The sailors and soldiers were chauffeured by local volunteers from USO headquarters in downtown Milwaukee to 107 homes

throughout Greendale for home-cooked dinners. Afterward, the servicemen were treated to a dance, a variety show staged by 13 local high school girls and a buffet supper at the Community Building.

Some 150 local girls, required to be at least 17 years old, signed up to be dance partners. The total cost of the party to the defense council was less than $15, according to Rae Getter, who

chaired the entertainment committee.

With many men off serving their country, Greendale felt the shortage of wartime labor.

On a September Sunday afternoon in '42, some two dozen residents swarmed to the nearby Van Alstine farm in cars, trucks and trailers for an old-fashioned "mow-down".

They came as a cooperative group, not to pick up their milk,

FARM HELP was hard to come by in '42 with men off to war. Farms like this surrounded Greendale back then.

but to help Tom Van Alstine get in feed crops for his cattle. Van Alstine now had only one farmhand, and he was worried about finishing the job in time.

Using his cutter equipment, they soon had harvested three of his four cornfields and hauled the silage into his barn. Afterward, Tom's wife set out an old-time thrashin' dinner for the "cornhuskers", complete with roast pork, fried chicken, mashed potatoes, beans and pumpkin pie.

The group's good deed spawned similar efforts by other residents. More than 50 men and women took up the good cause, helping village farmers get in their crops on Sundays, receiving home-cooked meals in return.

Carpooling Took on Urgency

As the war wore on, carpooling to jobs in Milwaukee took on real urgency. Residents took turns driving, and for a small sum they accepted passengers who had no available car. The recommended contribution was a dollar a week for round-trips and 50¢ for a week of one-way rides.

Organizing the work-shift hours at various companies was a formidable volunteer undertaking. *The Greendale Review* published three pages of detailed schedules in its November 18, 1942 edition. The pages listed the names and addresses of car owners, their employers' names and addresses grouped by proximity, and the hours the drivers left and returned to Greendale.

The cost of the national war effort meant an increase in work hours for employees handling the village's services. They were put on a 44-hour weekly schedule without more pay. The move was necessitated by the Farm Security Administration's budget cut for the Greenbelt communities.

At the same time, village ser-

PLENTY OF HELP showed up at Tom Van Alstine's farm on a Sunday afternoon. Two dozen Greendalers helped him harvest corn, put up silage and help with the evening milking. Later, Mrs. Van Alstine served an old-time farm dinner.

vice employees went "on the clock", punching in and out on a time clock installed in the service building.

The closer tabs on employee work schedules didn't dampen their patriotic ardor. Genevieve Molthen, village clerk, reported that every worker signed a pledge card authorizing a payroll deduction for defense stamps.

Students and faculty at Greendale School were also doing their bit. A "savings bank" had been set up at the school to encourage students to develop good saving and spending habits. It was decided that discontinuing the bank project during wartime and encouraging students to invest instead in defense stamps would be their patriotic contribution toward winning the war.

Meanwhile, the Greendale Defense Council continued recruiting volunteers for service on various committees, including draft registration, auxiliary fire and police, blood donations and community safety.

Within 2 months, nearly 20% of the village's adults—more than 300 persons—had been interviewed and assigned various defense-related tasks. More than 100 Greendale women were sewing, knitting and rolling bandages.

Helped Make Bandages

"I would help my mom and her friend roll bandages when I was 10 or 11," recalls Roberta Henrichs, who was an Eilers girl back then. "We had to be just perfect and make the bandages square. We wore a white dress and a white cap that had a little red cross on it. I felt I was doing my part for the war."

"We bought our own yarn and knitted the mittens and caps at home," adds Evelyn Truppe.

Another 100 or so residents enrolled in first aid training. And members of the Greendale Rifle Club started a civilian marksmanship course, teaching the care and proper firing of a gun.

NEARBY FARMS provided early residents with a close look at agriculture.

Why Kids Were Scared to Swim in Scout Lake

IN OCTOBER 1943, the government leased—without charge—a 23-acre wildlife and forest preserve to the Greendale Boy Scouts for a camp. The area on Highway 36, south of Grange Avenue, was well wooded and an "ideal site for the Scouting activities of both boys and girls". Called Demien's Lake, it later became known as Scout Lake.

Jack Murdaugh remembers Scout Lake being accessible by a dirt road, and recalls his one brave night venture there. "The lake was chained off, but we got a key from the police chief and fished the lake off a flimsy raft until midnight."

Jim Curtin says kids never thought of going swimming in Scout Lake. "It just never caught on with the kids," he surmises, "maybe because it wasn't real visible. Besides, the priest's house was just up the hill, and we didn't want to play around there."

The priest was Father Spangler, then pastor of St. Alphonsus, who lived in the Higer family farm-house for a time. The lake could be seen from there.

Perhaps more daunting was a story that circulated again and again among early residents: Supposedly a farmer drove his horse and wagon out onto the ice on Scout Lake one winter and broke through the ice. The body of the farmer was never recovered, it was said, nor was his horse or wagon.

"Yes, I've heard that story many times, too, over the years," recalls pioneer Bernie Schroedl. "But no one has ever been able to prove that it really happened. I think it was to keep us kids away."

Notwithstanding that mystery and Scout Lake's remoteness, school and church organizations were subsequently invited to use the facility, which was then called "New Camp Greendale". A lodge and cabins were later erected as camping quarters.

THE "MYSTERY" about Scout Lake (see story above) had many kids too scared to swim there in early years.

CHAPTER 29

War Sparked 'Garden Community' Tag

"VICTORY GARDENS" were planted by people across the country as part of the war effort. Greendalers eagerly joined the cause when the program was announced, with 125 families indicating their intention to plant "war gardens", as some of the locals called them.

The gardens sprouted up on vacant land in and around the village. "It seemed everybody had one," recalls Dick Lenten. "Ours was where St. Alphonsus is now.

"We'd put garbage cans on a wagon, fill 'em up with water from a hose, then haul the wagon to the garden, where we'd scoop the water into buckets and go along the rows, watering the plants."

A major victory garden site was on the north side of West Grange Avenue (now the site of Southridge Shopping Center). "I signed up for a double plot there, 50 by 50 feet," Ellis Brown says.

The government also convert-

ed into garden plots a huge tract of farmland occupying the area where Greendale High School now stands.

"I tended one of those gardens," chimes in Leo Hoyer. "At noon, I'd run down from my job at the post office to see if anything was coming through the ground," he says. "It was such a thrill for me. You could really raise a lot of stuff on a half-acre plot."

John Miller grew tomatoes on open land next to the present post

office. Many residents will remember it as the site of a Sentry food store. At the time, that land adjoined the village tennis courts and horseshoe pits.

The victory gardens weren't free. "We had to pay something like 50¢ for our plot. While that was quite a bit in those days, it was still a bargain," says Dick Lenten.

"Besides, the municipal sewage people did us a big favor. They'd bring their sludge for

VICTORY GARDENS were abundant in 1940 on north side of Grange Avenue. These gardens are where Southridge Shopping Center is now.

BACKYARD GARDENS produced food for occupants of "originals" in 1942.

fertilizing, and we'd shovel it into the garden."

Art and Leona Krueger had a large victory garden at the St. Alphonsus site. "It was right in the middle of where the playground is now," Leona notes.

" I remember the year I canned 400 quarts from our produce," says Leona. "With our growing family, I couldn't afford to buy canned goods, so that garden was very good to us."

But home canning was not without its risks. Canning beans proved to be a bang-up project for Leona.

"As I was moving the pressure cooker filled with eight jars, one exploded, and I dropped the rest! Glass flew all over; pieces even embedded themselves in the ceiling beams across the room! Luckily, it all missed my eyes."

And Mrs. William Schultz, who lived on Avena Court, was processing peaches in the oven when they blew up. "There were peaches all over the place," she said. The stove was badly damaged, but again, luckily, no one was injured.

So many Greendalers were busily preserving the output of their gar-dens that the idea of a "community canning center" was proposed by a special committee of the Greendale Garden Club, after meeting with an agronomist of the War Food Administration and Community Manager Kroening. A half dozen such centers were already operating elsewhere in the nation.

Kroening suggested a barn on Clover Lane could be used, and he offered to install the equipment, which would cost about $1,000.

Questionnaires were distributed, and the tabulation showed 172 vil-

> *"Greendale's housewives had canned an average of 185 quarts of food..."*

lage housewives were in favor of a centrally located center, while 75 were opposed...155 respondents wanted the center operated as a co-operative service at cost; 26 were opposed.

Asked whether the canning should be done under the guidance of an experienced worker, 67 were in favor, 56 preferred to do it on their own. Uncovered, too, was the fact that Greendale's housewives had canned an average of 185 quarts during the previous season.

Mrs. Allan Haslam, who lived in the rural section of Greendale, was in favor of a centralized canning unit. She contended it would take care not only of the farmers' surplus fruits and vegetables, but could provide storage for their meat and poultry.

Mrs. Howard Gregg, of Arbutus Court, said she canned 900 quarts the previous summer for her family of six.

"I used the hot water method—where you boil your food for several hours at a time," she explained. "Having all the burners on the stove going at the same time, I found it impossible to prepare hot food for my family because the stove was in use for canning."

Beyond this flurry of interest, the centralized canning center never materialized for lack of financial backing, and the women continued to do their own canning.

On the other hand, the benefits and satisfaction of gardening had caught the fancy of many residents and is believed to be responsible for the "Greendale—The Garden Community" tag the village proudly exhibits at its entrances today.

Villagers Play "War Games"

During the war, Greendale even became a practice "military objective".

The community's tranquillity was disrupted on a May weekend in 1942 when the third battalion of the Wisconsin State Guard staged war maneuvers in and around the village. The guardsmen bivouacked at a CCC Camp in nearby Whitnall Park and endured a typical army meal called "slumgullion".

The "invasion" began Saturday evening with so-called "retreat" ceremonies at the village's flagpole. "A goodly crowd of Greendalers hurried through their supper dishes to observe the event," reported *The Greendale Review*.

The action on Sunday was described by Co-Editor Joseph Pettit:

"Taking up positions astride Grange Avenue, west of 76th Street, the red troops impersonated the invading forces and prepared to stave off the attack of three companies of the third guard battalion under the blue banner.

"Several score of Greendale residents hurried another meal to be on hand along the line of attack. And some, including this weary observer, tramped the whole route across field and stream, up hill and down, until the red unit surrendered on the bank of the Root River near Loomis Road.

"War hazards such as land mines, poison gas and machine gun nests

were simulated by flares, smudge pots and firecrackers and were identified by large signs for the benefit of the spectators.

"Cool water for aching feet was much in demand after the surrender and march back to camp, both for the troops and overzealous Greendalers who had trailed them."

If the war maneuvers weren't enough, blackouts and air raid tests were vivid reminders of the war's impact.

At the signal, residents were to dim the headlights if they were in a car, or if they were at home, turn off all lights visible outside unless blackout curtains were drawn. Streetlights were turned off until the all clear sounded.

Local air wardens distributed "V" stickers to each home. Prominently displaying such a sticker in a window indicated the family was complying with all restrictions of the Victory Campaign.

In the words of one campaign pamphlet, changing meat-buying habits to include more poultry and fish "would assure our allies, our troops and our home workers of enough food to fight and win."

SCHOOLCHILDREN visit living quarters of CCC Camp at Whitnall Park in 1936 (top). Many men lived there.

STILL STANDING after all these years is welcoming sign at Loomis and Grange (right), constructed in 1944.

LITTLE WONDER Greendale became known for its flower gardens, with backyard abundance in these two photos.

THE TRADITION has continued—a "Garden Gazing Walk" annually invites backyard tours of Greendale's originals.

CHAPTER 30

Residential Expansion Begins

AS FAR BACK as December of 1938, the Farm Security Administration (FSA) had considered allowing private development of as many as 600 additional homes in remaining areas of Greendale.

At that point, only 572 of the planned 750 homes had been built, utilizing only several hundred of the 3,410 acres that the government had purchased. Most of the land was still occupied by the small farms surrounding the village.

The proposed new building sites on some 200 acres, with all improvements in place, were mainly along Southway, at the south end of the village.

That plan was abandoned due to the government's budget shortage, and in May of 1940, the FSA announced it would accept proposals from private builders to construct an additional 200 homes. They would be one- and two-story units with two or three

MORE HOMES were proposed in area surrounding originals in early '40s.

bedrooms, costing between $4,500 and $5,000.

Under the plan, the builders would lease the land for 99 years. Prospective residents could then either buy or lease the units from the builders, with no government involvement.

Also as early as 1940, the FSA began to change its mind about continuing to be the "landlord" for the Greenbelt communities, including Greendale.

FSA officials met with the Greenbelt, Maryland Citizens Association to explore whether the residents of that sister community would be interested in building private homes there.

That approach grew out of efforts by the Greenbelt group to set aside the government's policy of forcing residents to move from the community when their wage and salary increases lifted their annual income

above the maximum income level.

The committee proposed such residents be allowed to stay, but pay increased rent. As an alternative, it suggested that such families, if they wished, be allowed to build their own homes in the village.

Commenting on this momentous development, Greendale Community Manager Sherwood Reeder responded, "This discussion in Greenbelt parallels thinking and discussion here in Greendale," according to a report in *The Greendale Review* of February 7, 1940.

"We are keeping in touch with developments in the matter, and the suggestion has been made that the Greendale Citizens Association organize a similar committee to study the problem and bring forth recommendations.

"Due to the current policy, this community has already lost some

PRIME SPACE was still available in the late 1940s, as evidenced by this aerial view. The Village Hall can be seen in top center. There were no buildings on east side of Broad Street, and large barn still stood at end of Clover Lane.

families, whose members were making valuable contributions to community life and activities. There are prospects of losing others who would be missed.

"There are many now living here and others who would like to live here, but cannot because of the income restrictions. There is room for expansion, and the community would benefit if private development of housing could be undertaken," Reeder concluded.

Shortly afterward, the Greendale Citizens Association formed a Home Building Committee to develop a plan for home ownership.

A *Milwaukee Journal* news story in August of that year noted, "It was felt in official circles that outright sale or transfer of the model towns would lessen federal connection and would ensure a greater degree of self-government and individual responsibility."

Not long after, a group of Milwaukee investors made a bid for Greendale, but the effort came to naught. In the ensuing months, several Milwaukee area news stories stirred speculation about whether existing Greendale homes would be sold to individuals.

Reeder felt compelled to address the rumors, stating that in his opinion, the sale of present Greendale homes to individuals would not be practical. The design of the multiple units and the general layout of the village plan didn't lend themselves to such individual sales.

"The one idea that has seemed most likely," Reeder said, "is the transfer to a public housing authority or, where none exists, to a non-profit corporation that would operate in a way similar to a housing authority. Plans are still being studied, and although nothing has been definitely decided, I anticipate a decision may be made in the near future," he added.

"In whatever plan may be ultimately worked out, every effort will be made to ensure the continuation of the project for the purposes for

> ## *"Greendale tenants need have no fear their houses will ever be sold to anyone..."*

which it was originally intended. I feel certain that the welfare of the Greendale tenants will be given primary consideration."

In February 1943, the situation was further muddled. A flyer, author unknown, was distributed throughout the village, announcing that a meeting would be held in the Community Building on Tuesday the 23rd.

Subjects for discussion, according to the notice, would include election of village officers, explanation of war rationing and "individual home ownership and information on new leases (if obtainable)". One adult member of each family was requested to attend.

Walter Kroening, now village manager, immediately responded with an open letter to all Greendale residents, denying that his office had distributed the flyer.

"On the matter of individual home ownership," Kroening stated, "Greendale tenants need have no fear that their homes will ever be sold to anyone. It was not contemplated at the time of the construction of Greendale, nor is it now contemplated. If and when any changes in existing rental policies are decided upon, the residents will be promptly advised by the Management."

Kroening's words regarding "existing rental policies" proved to be the "first shoe". The "second shoe" was dropped in April '43.

HALE PARK EAST was one of the earliest developments, as homes sprouted up along 51st Street and beyond.

SMALLER HOMES like those above began showing up on the fringes of Greendale when this photo was taken in 1961.

LARGER HOMES like those below sprouted up quickly in new "Overlook Farms" area developed west of 76th Street.

CHAPTER 31

Greendalers Go on 'Rent Strike'

IN APRIL 1943, the Federal Public Housing Authority announced it was increasing rents in Greendale and the other two Greenbelt Towns. The reasoning behind the plan was that residents now earning higher incomes in wartime employment—which exceeded original federal limits—could be allowed to continue to live in Greendale while paying a proportionately larger rent.

"Four Bombs Hit Greendale" was the banner headline for a front-page editorial in *The Greendale Review*, which noted, "We anticipated an adjustment of our rents upward, a moderate increase, say, up to $5 or even $6 a month. But nothing like the actual verdict, which increases some of the rents $14 per month!"

The highest home rental under the revision would be $46 a month. The Greendale Citizens Association, which had lapsed into inactivity over the previous months, was re-energized and called a public hearing to get res-

idents' views on the new rent schedule.

The outcome of that highly vocal meeting was a resolution sent to President Roosevelt, requesting that rents be kept at the level set in his executive order of the previous March. Association board members sent copies of the resolution to senators, congressmen and newspapers.

The village's Board of Trustees passed a similar resolution at its

May meeting, in effect siding with the association in its protest.

In a later joint meeting, the trustees and the Citizens Association board voted unanimously to recommend a "rent strike"— urging tenants to refuse to pay their rent due June 1 until the matter was clarified.

The threat put Walter Kroening squarely in the middle. On the one hand, he could sympathize with the residents as village manager

SOME "ORIGINALS", as first homes were called, were built among huge trees, like this one on Apricot Court.

elected by the Village Board. On the other hand—serving as the federal government's paid representative—he was obligated to serve notice that tenants refusing to pay their rents would be evicted.

Kroening's first take on the rent strike was that it wasn't as serious as organizers were making it sound. After all, more than a third of the tenants—230 out of 635—had already signed new contracts for the increased rentals.

That may have been misleading, because the majority—the other two-thirds—would be affected as their leases expired at later dates. And of that majority, more than 400 tenants decided to take the matter to court for what the Citizens Association attorney termed "a friendly determination".

To finance a legal fund for the court appeal, residents voted to contribute $1 per family. An assessment of $2 per family was pushed by some more vocal opponents, but it was decided to hold off on that until more funds were needed.

A week later, in early June of 1943, Kroening and five village trustees piled into a government station wagon and drove to Washington to personally present their disapproval to the assistant commissioner of the National Housing Agency.

Their trip was in vain. Kroening reported back that the federal government couldn't be swayed and

> *"The village manager and five trustees piled into a government station wagon and drove to Washington..."*

would stick to its new rent policy. He also noted that, by then, only 17 families had refused to pay the increases and faced eviction.

Complicating the uproar were eviction suits filed by the federal government in federal court in Milwaukee against six families who refused to pay the higher rents, even though they'd signed leases containing the new rent policy.

LARGE BACK WINDOWS allowed parents to keep an eye on their children.

But Kroening also had some "good news". Because of a "book-keeping change" coincident with the shifting of authority to the National House Agency, he said, each Greendale family's water and electric rates were being reduced by $1 to $1.50 a month.

That news hardly slowed the rising opposition to the government's rent edict.

On June 21, the Citizens Association held another meeting, at which residents were again told that the trustees' trip had come to naught. It became evident to many that the federal government's preoccupation with the war had pushed Greendale's rent hassle to the back burner.

The controversy churned along the rest of the summer, gradually losing steam as some families refused to sign leases and moved out. Most others gave up the struggle and signed. Meanwhile, the court cases were either dropped or decided in favor of the government.

GREENDALE GALS in 1939. Enjoying a sunny "washday" Monday were (from left to right) Marilyn Koschin, Barbara Tarnowski, Glonja Koschin and Gloria Tarnowski.

ROLLING HILLS of 14 farms were turned into a charming village. This view looks south on Clover Lane. Notice how backs of houses face street and are set close to the curb.

RELUCTANT HONOR? Tommy Glynn and Donna Marie Mason, both 2, were "First Master and Missy of Greendale" in 1942. That close-up megaphone may have scared Tommy!

GREAT PICNIC SITE. Families gathered often in Willow Park (below), now known as Pioneer Park. Take note of how open the surrounding area is in this 1939 photo.

CHAPTER 32

Emotions Settle Down, Rally Held

DESPITE ALL THE TURMOIL in 1943, Greendale's neighborly and patriotic spirit remained intact. On a September evening, the village held a huge War Bond Rally at the Community Building.

More than 900 persons attended the ceremonies and signed up for war bonds in amounts ranging from $100 to $1,000. In all, villagers contributed a total of more than $22,000.

For their generosity, they were treated to song solos and duets, piano selections, square dances and hula dances, band numbers accompanied by three majorettes, and speeches by visiting veterans, topped off by a Gay Nineties Review performed by the Greendale Varietee Club under the direction of Rae Getter.

To further rekindle community spirit in the wake of the failed rent strike, a number of residents—many of them pioneer families—formed the Greendale Civic Group. Ironically, the group included Walter Kroening.

LABOR DAY in village was marked by numerous flags, such as the one in this nice photo by John Vachon.

At its first meeting, members approved an action plan drafted by its Friendly Neighbor Committee aimed at "making the lives of all Greendalers more complete and satisfactory by strengthening and encouraging the many fine clubs and organizations in the village, and by attracting newcomers to community activities."

In a nostalgic vein, *The Green-dale Review* noted, "Early settlers here remember the first year in the village, when everyone went to everything and had a wonderful time. As the years went by, that initial enthusiasm waned. The 'husking bee and ice cream social' spirit phased out as the village assumed a more cosmopolitan way of living.

"At no time in Greendale's de-

velopment, however, in spite of uncomfortable situations and crises, have the residents failed to be good neighbors," the newspaper went on.

"Those who experienced illness, hardships and unexpected emergencies have found themselves surrounded by willing helpers and kind friends. 'Come in and have a cup of coffee' is practically a village byword.

"It is this spirit of neighborliness and friendship that the Civic Group hopes to use to weld the entire community together."

On the group's social agenda were monthly luncheon meetings to which newcomers received special invitations. The first was attended by some 350 residents.

They listened to short talks by Civic Group members who headed up seven activity areas, acquainting them with recreational, youth, civic service, religious, arts, business and public services. Attendees were encouraged to sign up for activities and organizations they were interested in.

There was at least one lingering effect of the rent strike, however— the growing sentiment that Village

Manager Kroening could not serve two masters. In fact, the board of trustees at one point suspended Kroening's annual salary of $1,200 for several months until they were notified their action was not legal and that he was legally entitled to hold both positions.

Kroening's dual role was finally resolved in the form of state legislation prohibiting federal employees from holding positions in local gov-

---

" 'Come in and have a cup of coffee' is practically a village byword…"

---

ernment. That was the ammunition the trustees needed. In January of 1947, the board dismissed Kroening and appointed its own village manager, Robert Eppley.

With Kroening continuing as the federal government's community manager, at a salary of $5,600 a year, Greendale was served by two managers until the federal government sold the village in 1953.

In 1944, the trustees raised their

MEMORIAL DAY services in '48 were held at the Alonzo Hauser statue, which honors the village's pioneers.

own salaries. They passed an ordinance establishing the village president's pay at $300 a year, up from $150. The trustees' annual pay was also doubled, from $120 to $240.

Meanwhile, the possibility that the federal government would give up its landlord role in the Greenbelt communities resurfaced in several ways.

At this point, fully understanding—and then adequately explaining the ultimate transition of Greendale from a government-owned community to a privately financed entity—is akin to struggling with a political Rubik's Cube.

The Village Board created an advisory committee to sound out the federal government on the idea. The committee was also charged with checking into an earlier proposal, when the Farm Security Administration had jurisdiction, to allow private builders to convert the remaining 3,000 acres of undeveloped land into building lots and, in turn, lease them for 99 years to persons who would build their own homes.

Art Marcus, a vocal advocate of private home ownership in the village, suggested his plan in this August 1944 letter to a Mr. Clayton, administrator of Surplus War Property in Washington:

"The proposal would be to sell to the Greendale Co-operative all lands, private dwellings and business enterprises. The Greendale Co-operative would in turn resell the homes to the people."

As for the unused land, he suggested selling it for the building of additional homes. Marcus further proposed that the village be able to purchase the streets, utilities and public buildings from the government through the sale of bonds.

Marcus' letter was referred to the Federal Public Housing Authority, which replied, "No conveyance of present homes is practicable until the project can be expanded as originally planned, and this is necessarily dependent on war conditions."

Kroening added this bit of hope for the future: "The Federal Public Housing Administration anticipates that after the war, private capital will

Robert Eppley

be interested in residential expansion and industrial development in the Greendale area, and that methods are being considered for overcoming any legal obstacles to sale or long-term lease of the land."

About the same time, Kroening announced that negotiations were under way to sell unused land to the village's first three churches—

St. Alphonsus Catholic Church, St. Luke's Lutheran Church and the Greendale Community Church.

The government sold St. Luke's an acre of land for $400 on the south side of Northway directly across from Arrowwood Street. The Community Church purchased a site for their church on the northwest corner of Clover Lane and Southway.

And St. Alphonsus acquired a 6-acre site on Highway 36, just south of Grange Avenue. There were two farmhouses on the site—one that became the church rectory and the other the nuns' convent.

On V-E Day, in May of 1945, Greendale joined the rest of the nation in memorializing the end of the war in Europe. The village's three churches collaborated in an evening community service in the Community Building. Places of business were closed all day, and at school, pupils attended special services in the gym.

SCOUTS PLACE WREATHS at foot of Alonzo Hauser statue. Directing them at left is Art Krueger.

135

PIPING GOOD TIME. Hundreds of men found employment in the construction of Greendale. Above are the plumbers, who took a break at the height of construction in 1937.

SAFETY CHECK. Greendale police were keenly involved in the lives of early residents. This boy has a fancy bike—with those baskets, he likely delivered newspapers.

CHAPTER 33

Government Sells Surrounding Land

AS THE VILLAGE MARKED its seventh year of existence, in May of 1945, the Federal Public Housing Administration (FPHA) suddenly showed an interest in selling the government's surplus land surrounding the three Green-belt Towns—particularly Green-dale.

Elbert Peets, the village's original designer, was hired to plan for an additional 3,600 homes, in clusters of four neighborhoods throughout the village. These homes would be privately built rather than government-built.

His plan became the blueprint for much of the contours of an expanded Greendale. In a notable departure from his 1936 plan, Peets created U-shaped streets—that is, parallel streets joined by a loop at one end and two openings onto main thoroughfares.

Greendale's Board of Trustees then approved two new subdivisions—the Clover Lane section south of the existing village, and Dahlia Hill to the west.

Testing the market for interest

REAL DEAL. Lots in the Clover Lane section went on sale for $800 in 1945.

in Greendale that same year, the FPHA offered 64 lots in the Clover Lane section for sale. The average lot size was approximately 9,700 square feet, and the price was about $800.

The government said this would be its only direct sale of land to individuals. Subsequent sales of lots and homes would be handled by private developers.

A Design Review Committee

would approve building plans for each house in the new development. The intent, the government said, was not to conform building designs to the village's original homes, but simply to avoid "poor architecture and poor placement" on the lots.

The first 2 weeks of the October sale of lots were set aside for purchases solely by veterans. The first buyer was Art Marcus. Fol-

137

THIS VACANT SITE? It's where St. Alphonsus Church is located today.

lowing the veterans' preference period, Greendale residents had next choice.

With the platting of the Clover Lane lots, the long-standing and popular ice rink there was abandoned in favor of a new rink at Catalpa and Dale Lanes, and the familiar shelter house was also relocated.

Sales started slowly, then picked up dramatically. A Milwaukee real estate company was soon doing a land-office business, selling 2- to 5-acre farms just outside the village, around Highway 36 and Edgerton Avenue and 43rd Street. These were sold to Greendale residents, presumably for larger home sites more so than to be farmed.

"Musical Chairs" Arrangement

The sale of larger lots was brisk for another reason. An important change in the government's rent policy for Greendale took place that year. Known as the "home exchange provision", it was a "musical chairs" arrangement designed to enable families to move to larger or smaller quarters within the village as their income and family circumstances changed.

The policy change, Kroening said, was intended "to take full advantage of our housing capacity and to furnish proper accommodations for growing families." The exchange was voluntary but could be enforced, Kroening noted, in line with the occupancy criteria established by the government.

Within the following year, some 30 families had moved to different units, including six in 1 day. Another

> *"Some residents had to move because their salaries now exceeded government standards…"*

er 60 families were on the "must move" list by the middle of 1947. The village's population count at that point was 2,810.

Milwaukee's celebration of its 100th birthday in July 1946 gave 8-year-old Greendale an excellent opportunity to showcase its virtues and brought more potential buyers to the area. Setting a theme of "Tomorrow's Town Today", the village entered two floats in Milwaukee's Centurama parade.

The first float, promoting Greendale as a garden city, was adorned with some 3,000 roses plus hundreds of petunias, marigolds and other flowers contributed by villagers from their gardens.

Seated aboard the float in an attractive floral arbor was 18-year-old Diane Gill, of Cardinal Court, reigning as Greendale Garden Queen.

She was escorted by seven flower attendants, girls ages 4 to 6 years—Patsy Patenaud, Ruth Schlueter, Barbara Brinkman, Sharon Wuchterl, Janice Bjorn, Diane Behne and Judy Zingler. Dressed as butterflies were Janice Lange and Patty Gregg.

A second float, accenting Greendale's farm heritage, was decorated with giant vegetables surrounded by hay and farm tools. Aboard were Jack Spratler and his "Corntassel Corner Band", along with Marlene Bansemer, Nancy Colter, Joni Napier, Nancy Hanel, Gloria Tarnowski and Beverly Koterman, all dressed as "farmerettes".

Erv Koenigsreiter filmed the floats and the queen with her court and promised a general showing at the theatre later.

Greendale was awarded the prize for the Best Municipal Float in Milwaukee County.

PARADES have always been popular in Greendale. "Garden Queen" on float above is Diane Gill (now Hones).

BEAUTIFUL DAY for a parade! The vintage car, straw hats and tractor towing a float help date the photo below.

PATH above is parallel to Grange between Apple Court and Arrowwood. Greendale's designer purposely made paths narrow so people would meet, talk and get to know each other.

BUSY 1961 Village Hall office staff includes (below, left to right) Marge Hanson, John Kuglitsch, Hedwig Tomczak, Caroline Brandt, Jerry Haag and Ed Kramer.

CHAPTER 34

New Businesses Come to Village

SOME BUSINESSES left Greendale in 1946, and others arrived in 1947. A familiar sight for the past 6 years disappeared from downtown in the summer of '46, as the Frank Specialty Company's lease expired on its dry goods store in the Mercantile Building.

The Greendale Co-operative Association took over operation of the store with a line of variety merchandise.

The following April, a new "face" appeared on Broad Street when Layton State Bank opened its office adjacent to the Greendale Theatre. Leo Betanski was appointed manager of the office.

In other enterprise activity, negotiations were begun to bring light industry to Greendale. An 8-acre tract on the west side of Loomis Road (the present site of the village's Industrial Park) was set aside. The first company to show interest said it would employ some 250 people.

In November, "Butch" and Allis Burns opened their Greendale Grill on Broad Street in quarters previously housing the Co-op's office, which had moved to the second floor of the Village Hall. The specialty of the house was "Butchburgers", plus hot ham and

GREENDALE'S 10th birthday is being celebrated by Ray Miller, Rachel Brinkman and Walter Kroening.

SOAP BOX DERBY was fun for drivers Gene Scham, Dick Eddy, Darrol Boyer, Carl Yors, Vic Woeste and Mickey Richter.

AND THE WINNER nears finish line, which appears to be at bottom of Northway. A big crowd turned out to watch in 1947.

rolls and other deli goodies offered on Sundays.

January 1947 was newsworthy for the major winter blizzard that paralyzed the greater Milwaukee area for the better part of some 21 days!

The snow started falling and continued until more than 23 inches were on the ground. Cars, trucks, buses and streetcars became mired in the white stuff until the area looked like one giant parking lot gone berserk.

Another bit of news in 1947 was the announcement from Community Manager Kroening that it was painting time again for the exterior of the original homes.

The good news was the paint would be "washable"—lead and oil paints would be used. The bad news was there would be no new color choices; only buff, which he said was so popular with the housewives.

"Technical restrictions, coupled with coverage ability, preclude a wider choice of colors," he explained.

Take Me Out to the Ball Game

Greendalers' keen interest in sports continued when the Recreation Department organized the Southwest Suburban Softball League. Teams were entered from Greendale, Hales Corners, Tess Corners, Waterford, Wind Lake, Mukwonago and West Allis. Robert Irvine, Greendale's new recreation director, offered to supply the umpires and equipment.

To keep pace with residents' ever-growing interest in baseball and softball, Brinkman Field was equipped with floodlights for night ball games, along with additional bleachers and an enlarged parking area.

In dedication ceremonies preceding a game the night of July 29, Mrs. George Brinkman, Greendale's first "first lady", switched on the floodlights in honor of her husband, for whom the field was named.

It was baseball at its best—exuding the kind of small-town love of the game that somehow bonded everyone in an exuberant spirit.

ROASTING HOT DOGS was a hit with these Scouts during a camp-out. Front, left to right: Don Silke, Ronald Campion, Bud Hill, Scott and Jerry Uelmen. Back, John Thoman, Carson Lunde, Scoutmaster Art Krueger and Don Uelmen.

"Haven't those ball games been a wonderful thing for our community?" commented a writer in *The Greendale Review*. "Certainly a grand way to spend an evening, rooting and cheering your team to win. Brother, there was really some

> *"For the first time since August 1938, the community's major voice was stilled..."*

cheering at some of those last games. In fact, there was so much noise some of the time, you couldn't hear the announcer."

The Fourth of July celebration in 1947 was sponsored by American Legion Greendale Post 416 and expanded to a 3-day event, promising to be the village's biggest Fourth of July celebration in the 9 years of its history.

Crowds of people from nearby communities, estimated at 10,000, poured into the village, jamming traffic on every street to witness a variety of events, including the State Amateur Bike Meet and an outstanding fireworks display.

A major youth event on the third day was the annual Coasting Classic, patterned after the National Soap Box Derby. Local youngsters gave their racing cars such speedy names as "Streak", "Speedwagon", "Juggernaut", "Rocket", "Flash" and "Bombshell". Their racetrack was Northway, from the top of the hill near Westway, and curving down into the village center.

Freddie Strong won first place for the fastest time in the entire event, 30.7 seconds. Just a whisker behind him, with a time of 30.8 seconds, was James Stranberg. The Legion contributed first- and second-place trophies, and local businesses contributed other prizes. Freddie and James' Scout den also won a traveling trophy.

The Legion sponsored the well-attended 3-day celebration to raise funds for their proposed Youth Memorial Building.

Unfortunately, whatever else would be happening in the village in the coming weeks and months would have to rely on word of mouth, rumor and sightings. For the first time since August 1938, the community's major voice was stilled.

The Greendale Review announced it was suspending publication for an indefinite period. The circumstances that had prompted it to cut back from weekly to bimonthly editions had not improved.

Several newspapers subsequently set up shop to report village developments. *The Greendale Post* published its first *Greendale Newspaper* on June 30, 1959. It was sold in March 1960, and the successor company increased its circulation to cover not only Greendale, but also Greenfield, Hales Corners and Franklin. It renamed its paper simply *The Post*.

Later, there were the *Greendale Times*, *Greendale News* and *Tri-Town News*. Finally, the current *Greendale Village Life* began publication in October 1960.

BIG ELM TREE on the east of Broad Street was the site of many activities, including this Scout camp in 1947.

CHAPTER 35

No Mayor for Greendale

ONE NOTABLE EVENT in 1948 was the decision whether Greendale should retain its "village manager" form of government or switch to either a city mayor/alderman form, and also more/less taxes versus less/more taxes, depending on which of the calculations voters were to believe.

More than 80% of eligible vil-

lage residents went to the polls on April 6, with 673 casting votes against the change and 195 voting for it.

The question of changing Greendale's status as a village has never again come to a vote.

Also in 1948, the issue was raised for the first time of whether the village should provide a full 4-

year high school education to its pupils. That would necessitate expanding the school to include 11th and 12th grades.

After first delaying a decision 3 weeks earlier, the Greendale School Board voted on June 10

SAY CHEESE. Graduating class of 1955 poses near 5-year-old school.

QUITE A PROJECT. Our staff wasn't able to find names of the Greendale students above, but teacher is "Mrs. Lange".

THE HELMETS of this Greendale High football team lead us to believe this photo was taken in the early '50s.

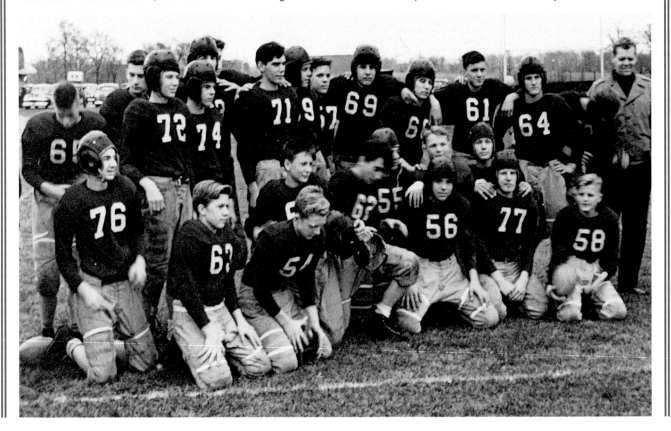

in favor of the expansion. To accommodate the expected larger student body, four of the larger schoolrooms and the music room were each partitioned into two rooms, and the second floor was reconfigured for high school classes.

The newly constituted high school held its first senior class graduation in 1950. Fifty-eight students received their diplomas.

Dan Casey enjoys his distinction as the first graduate of Greendale High School.

"I was one of two shorter guys at either end of the first row on stage of the auditorium. I was positioned there along with the shorter girls," Dan recalls of the June graduation ceremony.

"So I was the first name called and the very first person to receive a diploma from Greendale High School. Ever since I've been able to say I graduated 'first in my class'; but that's chronologically, not scholastically."

The present Greendale High School, at the foot of Broad Street and slightly to the west, was opened in January 1957. It was built in four stages. The initial unit, with a capacity for 300 to 400 students, was ready in 1956.

In 1957, the second construction phase enlarged the school by seven classrooms. A gym and manual arts classrooms were later added in the third phase, and the fourth unit was built west of the existing building.

New Business Environment

The commercial environment of the village began changing in 1948, as the government reassigned leases for its various businesses.

The changes were largely a disappointment for the Greendale Cooperative Association, which lost its leases and meant it no longer had authority to sublease the food store, variety store, theatre and barbershop. It did retain its leases on the Village Inn and Garage & Service Station.

Shortly thereafter, Clem and Dick Trimborn took over operation of the food store; Hilbert Drews, the

CHEERLEADERS ready to yell are Beverly Katerman and Joan Altman (front), Nancy Burns, Diane Casey and Dee Lee Haubrick (back).

CUTTING EDGE is ready to slice ceremonial cake float displayed in front of the Village Hall. The number on top suggests this was on the village's 10th birthday.

variety store; Orville Harris and Al Lodde, the barbershop; and Jerome Goderski replaced Erv Koenigsreiter as manager of the theatre. Koenigsreiter moved to Racine to manage a theatre there.

But soon after, Koenigsreiter responded to an offer from the private developers who had since acquired the theatre; he returned to Greendale to again manage the theatre he'd learned to love.

The second time around was not enough to save the theatre, which had fallen on hard times. Koenigsreiter pointed to rent increases and difficulties with film distributors as the main reasons. He closed the theatre for good in 1967.

In June of 1948, Greendale belatedly celebrated its 10th birthday. The official date was April 30, but the event was scheduled to coincide with the state of Wisconsin's 100th anniversary of its founding.

On the first day of the 3-day celebration, families living on Beaver Court were honored by having their street selected as the "Court of Honor" in a Street Beautification Contest. Greendale schoolchildren staged a colorful pageant titled "The Freedom Train".

A Founders Day dinner on Saturday evening in the school gymnasium was a centerpiece event of the celebration. It was attended by a notable group of dignitaries led by Sherwood Reeder, Greendale's first manager, who was guest speaker.

In the audience were Milwaukee Mayor and Mrs. Frank Zeidler and other city, county and state officials; also Walter Kroening, Elbert Peets and Fred Naumer were honored for their roles in Greendale's early planning. The guests dined on a fine turkey dinner with all the trimmings.

Eleanor Couldn't Make It

Eleanor Roosevelt, invited to attend, sent her regrets, saying she was unable to make plans because of current Human Rights Commission meetings.

Weekend speakers pointed out dramatic improvement in Greendalers' quality of living had taken place in those 10 years. A government analysis of the incomes of 545 village families showed the average

GREENDALE HIGH SCHOOL was built in four stages. The initial unit, which opened in 1956, had a capacity for 300 to 400 students. Photo taken in 1958.

family income had doubled in that period, from $1,695 in 1938 to $3,450 in 1948.

The figures included earnings of working wives, but not of the children. The greatest number of families—88—were in the $3,000 bracket, 20 families were in the $4,500 group and 60 families had incomes of up to $8,000 a year. The 47 remaining families in the study earned less than $3,000, and a few made as low as $1,500 a year.

Eventually, growing city slums and the national housing crunch that had accelerated with the return of veterans after World War II became the "magic" solution to the expansion of Greendale.

Available undeveloped land surrounding the community was eyed for relieving the housing shortage. The result was quick growth around the village's edges in a few short years.

CHAPTER 36

Greendale 'Originals' Go on Market

A MOMENTOUS announcement in 1948 reverberated throughout Greendale: Congress authorized the Housing and Home Finance Agency (HHFA) to dispose of the Greenbelt Towns—both the homes rented out by the government and the undeveloped land!

It did not specify a date for the sale. Immediately, at least three local groups began competing for the right to purchase Greendale.

A major player in the competition was the American Legion Community Development Corporation (ALCDC), incorporated as a nonprofit entity in 1947 to acquire Greendale and sell its homes and unused land to veterans.

Its bid was later amended to allow not only veterans but residents as well to buy or rent their present homes.

ALCDC was later backed by the Village Board and the city of Milwaukee, which invested $300,000 in the group.

Another veterans group, the Greendale Veterans Co-operative Homes Association (GVCHA),

also intended to purchase Greendale homes, then operate them as co-operative housing.

A third major player in the purchase competition was the Greendale Residents' Home Purchase Committee, which submitted a bid to the government to allow residents to buy the village on a "no-profit basis", with a down payment of 10% and a 30-year mortgage at 3-1/2% interest.

The members of this third group expressed the fear that a private firm could come into the village to "make a killing at the expense of the residents, forcing a lot of us out of Greendale". This home purchase committee eventually backed the GVCHA in its bid, along with the Greendale Citizens Association.

At one point, there was some sentiment for the ALCDC and the GVCHA to combine their efforts.

"It has been suggested that control of the developed area be given to the GVCHA," an editorial stated, "and that the city (Milwaukee) and the ALCDC control

LAND adjacent to the original homes found an eager market when offered.

development of the unused area. The merger would ensure veterans of low-cost homes, and importantly, it would ensure the present tenants of a fair chance of buying or renting their present homes."

The two groups did tentatively agree on just such a plan. However, the merger effort failed because Milwaukee's Common Council wanted assurance that Greendale would be annexed to the city.

When that didn't happen, the city of Milwaukee demanded return of the $300,000 it had invested in the ALCDC. And ALCDC and GVCHA themselves ultimately could not agree on any compromise proposal.

Finally, in an advisory referendum on August 23, 1949, more than 70% of the village's eligible voters overwhelmingly rejected the ALCDC plan.

They opted for the GVCHA, partly out of fear that the ALCDC plan would deprive them of a chance to purchase or continue renting their homes. They also feared it would open the door for Greendale to be annexed by Milwaukee.

Korean War Halted Process

By the beginning of 1950, it became evident that none of these groups would win government approval of their purchase plans. What's more, the outbreak of hostilities in Korea began occupying Washington's attention.

Soon after the Korean War began, President Harry Truman suspended efforts to dispose of all Greenbelt communities in case they might be needed for defense housing. Facing this and other challenges, the Public Housing Administration (PHA) decided to hold off trying to work out a sale of Greendale.

Subsequently, Greendale's Vil-

STAND CLEAR! As Greendale grew to its outskirts, it gradually became less rural. Many of the pioneers regretted seeing the barn and silo taken down on Clover Lane as signs of progress.

STRENKE BARN was also removed in 1962 from "Parcel 55" at the corner of Loomis Road and College Avenue.

lage Board set up a housing authority, which was permitted under state law. The move was aimed at persuading the PHA to sell the village to Greendale's housing authority.

The board's maneuver was challenged, however, on the grounds that the village wasn't experiencing a housing shortage—a necessary precondition for establishing a housing authority.

The controversy continued to escalate. The Village Board also tangled with the PHA over the board's use of rent payments for utility space and equipment.

When the controversy between the Village Board and the PHA became even more heated, Greendale's housing authority finally decided to take the matter to the courts. That proved pivotal. In 1951, the PHA decided the time commitment and adverse publicity of this issue being played out in court was the final straw.

It ordered Greendale to be sold—first the homes, then the undeveloped land around the village.

Thanks to efforts by Congressman Clement Zablocki, residents would have the first opportunity to buy their homes at a price to be set by an independent assessor. After that, homes not yet sold would be first offered to veterans, then to the general public.

The historic sale started in 1952. Selling the single homes was relatively simple. But the sale of multiple units wasn't resolved that easily.

The PHA decided that where residents of a row house could not agree on a group purchase, the individual units in the building would

---

"For the sale of multiple homes, tenants' names went into a hat…"

---

be sold by lottery. So the names of tenants from such multiple units went into a hat.

The family whose name was drawn had the option to buy the multiple unit it was living in. If it did, the other families occupying the unit would have a new landlord—that is, the tenant whose name had been drawn. Or they could choose to move, and a number of them did.

It was not a lottery that pleased everyone. Some 200 families were "losers". Others simply couldn't afford the price to buy their home or even make the down payment.

Dick Lenten's family lost out. "My mother didn't have the money to pay that $50 down. We didn't have a father living at home. I was in the Army, and Mother was still supporting my two brothers," he comments. "For us, it was a terrific amount of money. So she never bought the house."

The luck of the draw wasn't with Sigmund and Alice Tylenda, either. "We had to draw straws with Mrs. Kindel to see who would have the chance to buy our half of the unit," Sigmund recalls. "With my 'Irish luck', I lost. I was really disappointed. We loved Azalea Court."

Fortunately, Sigmund's luck soon changed. He learned that if your name was picked, you would be

EARLY PHOTO, taken in 1939, shows east side of Broad Street. Series of one-level stores was built here in 1958.

EXPANSION continued with additional "alphabetized" sections. This is the S section being built. College Avenue is on the left, and Highland View School is in the upper right corner of photo.

given an option of buying land in Greendale.

"There was a lot that I could see from our bathroom window. It was a playground then. I used to say, 'If they'd ever want to sell that, I'd buy it.' And when I was told by the village that I had first choice on any lot, I got that one for $1,500."

Christine Kindel was one of the winners. "There were four apartments, and we had the chance to buy two of them when our name was drawn," she says. "We paid $11,000 for the two units."

Leo Hoyer vividly recalls when his family lost out in the drawing for the double unit they were living in. "But since some people didn't have the money to buy the single house they were living in, there were some left over," he relates. "My name was drawn for one of those, and I got a single home on Angle Lane."

Evelyn Truppe still remembers her anxiety about the lottery draw for their multi-unit home on Butternut Court. "I chewed my nails to next to nothing, worrying about whether we would get it," she says. "As it turned out, the other tenants were newlyweds and an older couple, and neither wanted to buy it. We paid about $7,000 for it."

Art and Leona Krueger, still living in one part of the double unit they won the opportunity to buy in the lottery, recall, "We paid the very expensive price of $14,625 for it. We had to pay $1,500 down."

Paper Route Helped

Bernie Schroedl and his sister made a necessary sacrifice so their parents could buy their home.

"They needed $1,000. At the time, some gentleman, who was a wealthy individual, was giving people $1,000 on a 3- or 4-year note. But the interest had to be paid each year," Bernie explains.

"I had a paper route, and my oldest sister was working at Drews variety store. I was saving for a car, but the house came first. Together, we somehow managed $8,800 for a three-bedroom original!"

Marian Prey says her family was fortunate. "We were in a single home and were able to buy it for $8,500," she notes. "When we sold it in 1965, we got $13,500 for it."

George Weimer and his family, too, got first choice on the single home they were living in. "We had six children. Where else could you go with them?" he comments.

"We paid $8,575," George remembers. "For us and many others, these original Greendale homes certainly were a good deal."

CHAPTER 37

Expanding While Retaining Tradition

WHILE the Public Housing Administration had made the decision to sell Greendale's housing in 1951, it decided to retain the undeveloped lands for the time being.

But in October 1952, the PHA changed its mind—it decided to put up for sale the 2,236 acres of land still in government ownership. The municipal and commercial buildings of the village center would be sold separately.

The land and buildings were an attractive buy for anyone who could afford it, and they particularly drew the attention of a number of real estate speculators from around the country.

Fortunately for Greendale, a small group of Milwaukeeans formed the Milwaukee Community Development Corporation (MCDC). Organizing the group were four prominent and respected men from the Milwaukee area: Richard Herzfeld, board chairman of Boston Store; William Roberts,

president of Allis-Chalmers; Francis Trecker, president of Kearney-Trecker Corporation; and Louis Quarles, senior member of the Quarles, Herriott and Clemons law firm.

This group saw Greendale as a good business investment and also as a unique experiment that should be developed in keeping with its Greenbelt planning principles. So in 1953, the MCDC

bought all of the undeveloped land in and around the village as well as its stores and public buildings.

They immediately employed Elbert Peets to devise a master plan for Greendale. Peets' plan, completed in 1957, represented an update of his 1945 design.

Each new residential neighborhood would have 1% to 20% of its area in parks. At the request of the

THE BUYERS. Four members of this group of businessmen purchased Greendale's undeveloped land, all its public buildings and stores from the federal government in 1952.

153

APARTMENT COMPLEX added to Greendale's expansion in 1961. These are Tower Apartments on Tower Road and Elberton Avenue. Vacant land with sign behind apartments is future site of Our Shepherd Lutheran Church.

MCDC, residential areas were expanded and the greenbelt decreased to coincide with the boundaries of the Root River Parkway.

In 1958, the MCDC sold the Village Hall, then valued at $150,000, to the Village Board for $55,000. Through the group's careful and intelligent guidance, Greendale began expanding to its current parameters, modernizing yet very carefully retaining its sense of tradition.

New homes soon began occupying the undeveloped land and gradually changed the look of Greendale. Reflecting the changing times and tastes, they were quite different in design from the "originals" that formed the A, B, C and D sections.

As each new addition was built, a homeowners association was organized to care for the common green space. Even so, for some of the pioneers, the growth was a bit hard to take.

Recalls Jack Murdaugh, "Although the village kept much of its original charm, a few of the original settlers were not happy with the changes that were taking place."

The '50s and '60s saw the birth of subdivisions such as Sherwood Heights, Edgerton Highlands and Lake Highlands. Edgerton High-

lands was chosen for the Milwaukee area Parade of Homes in 1958.

The Milwaukee Community Development Corporation also kept up the tradition of giving attention to recreation facilities in the village. In 1958, they formed a committee with a group of interested residents to plan a "Community Club". The

> *"In 1956, homes began taking shape on the rolling farmland west of 76th Street..."*

MCDC leased to the club a 7-acre piece of land for the facility south of the Sherwood Heights subdivision and adjacent to the Root River Parkway. The lease fee was initially $1, then the MCDC eventually donated the land outright.

"We envision it as a hub for village social activities and athletics, with emphasis on family participation," said MCDC's Vice President LeRoy Riegel.

Membership in the club was restricted to Greendale residents. Facilities included a large swimming pool, tennis courts, a bathhouse,

wading pool and tot yard for preschoolers. The club has fared well ever since. With the baseball/softball fields and basketball courts that were later developed adjacent to it, this Community Club has seen big use by Greendale families.

Construction in Greendale continued to boom. In 1950, the village's population stood at 2,752. By 1960, it had reached 6,843.

Allow Apartments?

During this same period, there was much debate among village officials and residents on the issue of zoning to permit apartments. A "yes" vote finally supported the zoning, and multi-family apartments began appearing throughout the village.

The first "apartment belt" was on Crocus Court, to the southwest of downtown stores, and was a major convenience for senior-age residents.

Other apartment units began changing the landscape in the Canterbury Heights area near the village water tower. The Overlook Garden

Apartments on the southeast corner of Parkview Road and South 76th Street soon took shape, followed by the Lake Highlands Apartments along Loomis Road and Southway, and the Greenway Apartments at the north edge of the original village.

Overlook Farms Take Shape

The home building boom shifted dramatically to the west in 1956, crossing South 76th Street. Overlook Farms and Overlook Farms West replaced rolling farmlands, but there was never a doubt that the projects would stop short of absorbing the noted Trimborn Farm.

Trimborn Farm dates back to 1851, the year Werner Trimborn started a lime business. With lime being a necessary ingredient in mortar and plaster, his farm became a major producer for the next 40-some years. The lime was hauled down an angular northeastern street, now Forest Home Avenue, to downtown Milwaukee.

Many of the city's buildings were built with that lime. Production reached a million barrels shipped

TRIMBORN FARM was never threatened by Greendale's expansion. Built prior to the Civil War, the farm's "beehive kilns" (right) produced lime for many of Milwaukee's buildings. Its barn (below), built in 1920s, is touted as the largest stone barn in Wisconsin. The farmhouse (top), built with Milwaukee Cream City Brick, is still sturdy.

BOYHOOD HOME of Jeremiah Curtin is well maintained. At left is stack kiln that was formerly north of Grange Avenue.

annually in the 1880s to Milwaukee and other parts of the Midwest.

When the demand for lime began to decline in the 1900s, the farm went into the dairy business. Ownership of the farm was passed to Theodore and Clara Vollmer.

In 1928, local businessman Thomas Saxe purchased the farm, using it as sort of a personal resort. He sold it to the government in 1936, when it became part of the government's acquisition of land for the Greendale project.

In 1980, the farm was turned over by developers to the Milwaukee County Park System, which turned it into a park. To preserve the history of the once-prospering art of turning limestone into lime, the farm has been designated a historic landmark, known as Trimborn Farm Park.

Under Milwaukee County Park System's continuing ownership, volunteers—first the Park People and currently the Milwaukee County Historical Society—have operated the farm, attracting many visitors.

The barn, home and unique lime kilns on the property plus its fascinating history make Trimborn Farm an ideal site for the annual Harvest of Arts & Crafts, school field trips and other events.

Another surviving memento of the history of Greendale is the Jeremiah Curtin home, situated just east of Trimborn Farm Park. The limestone cottage was built in 1847 with stone from a quarry, owned by Jeremiah's uncle. It was located across the road, which is now Grange Avenue.

Jeremiah Curtin came to Wisconsin from Detroit with his parents in 1837, when he was 2 years old. After graduation from Harvard University, he gained fame as an author, diplomat and linguist.

One of his noted accomplishments was translating into English the book *Quo Vadis* by Polish author Henryk Sienkiewicz. The Curtin home has been carefully preserved and hosts hundreds of literary tourists each year.

CHAPTER 38

Light Industry Firms Courted

AS GREENDALE'S population continued to grow, the Milwaukee Community Development Corporation (MCDC) began an effort to attract light industry to the area, so village residents could work near home.

With this in mind, the MCDC created an industrial park along Loomis Road (Highway 36) in 1957. Roads were graded on the site, and water and sewer facilities were installed on 18 lots.

During a 2-year period, three companies—Precision Molded Products, Louis Allis Research Center and Adam Products—had erected buildings there. The MCDC said it was also studying other village areas for light manufacturing development.

To encourage further construction of light industrial buildings in the area, the MCDC entered into an agreement with an industrial developer, Roxboro Inc., in December 1959. Roxboro mailed some 5,000 brochures, hoping to attract small manufacturing plants, warehousing firms and truck terminals.

At one point in its promotions, Roxboro announced an $8 million development plan that called for a million-dollar hotel-motel building and restaurant just north of the Industrial Park to be started in 1961. However, the project never got off the ground because of village zoning restrictions.

The Industrial Loop was never expanded beyond its original 48 acres, according to Donald Fieldstad, who was village manager

ALLIS-CHALMERS built three large research buildings at the corner of 60th and Grange Avenue in 1958.

157

BEFORE AND AFTER. At left is the somewhat run-down Allis-Chalmers site that was left vacant for over 7 years. Above is Reiman Publications' headquarters after the site was renovated.

then, because a 1974 change in industry tax laws made residential development more valuable than industrial development at the time.

A major industrial client did set up shop in 1958 on the north edge of the village. Allis-Chalmers constructed three large buildings on some 29 acres at the corner of Grange and South 60th Street. The move required the relocation of the Thor Nicolaisen home to another

site east along South 51st Street.

Allis-Chalmers had won a large government contract. The site housed a nuclear power research laboratory, offices and a large manufacturing facility.

The enterprise prospered for about a decade, employing as many as 500 people at one point, working on lucrative contracts with power plants around the nation.

But, gradually, hard times set in,

employment was cut back year after year, and the entire operation was finally shut down in 1973.

The buildings remained empty for over 7 years and fell into disrepair; the three structures were badly in need of painting, and tall grass and weeds overtook a good deal of the site. Greendalers became increasingly concerned as the "ghost buildings" and grounds became an eyesore at the village's entrance.

Finally, in 1980, Roy Reiman, founder of Reiman Publications, purchased the property for his growing business of publishing country-oriented cooking and nostalgia magazines and books, as well as a large direct-mail catalog business that required warehouses.

Rehabbing and converting the

buildings was a major undertaking, Reiman recalls. For example, he was amazed to learn the main office building had *no insulation*!

There were two huge furnaces in the facility, and they'd been put to big use. Cheap energy back in 1958 had made it less costly to heat than insulate the interiors in all kinds of weather. So, it could be zero outside and 70 degrees inside by simply firing up those two furnaces.

The second or middle building on the site was three stories high with a huge crane in it that Allis-Chalmers had used for its engineering needs. The publishing company had no use for that crane, nor did it need a building that high.

So, Reiman's CFO, Norbert Whittle, found an engineering firm that was highly interested in that expensive crane. He bartered with the firm and gave them the crane for free—in return for their lowering the roof to a two-story level.

Much Too Big at First

In the beginning, the facility was too large for Reiman Publications' needs. The third building wasn't even needed.

"At first, we were sort of rattling around in the first two buildings," Reiman remembers. "Those two structures provided much more space than we needed at the time."

A group of a dozen doctors showed interest in the third building, and Reiman was eager to rent it to them. Negotiations on a 10-year lease strung on for months, as the doctors had difficulty deciding what shape the facility would take. Finally, they insisted on something that became a deal-breaker.

They would only sign the lease if there could be an east entrance to the facility off of Loomis Road. The village engineer at the time, Nick Paulos, would have no part of that—he contended an entrance/exit so close to Grange Avenue would be a safety hazard.

So the deal fell through, and at first Reiman was disappointed. A few months later, as his business

Roy Reiman

continued rapid growth, he was relieved. The company's expanding needs took over the entire third building. And in the years hence, it has made several sizable additions to all three buildings to accommodate the mail-order catalog division,

a new cooking school division and a growing group tour business.

The company renovated the grounds, too. A landscaping firm was hired to turn the 29 acres into a corporate park, with berms, new trees, a plethora of flowers, a pond with a fountain, bridges, a gazebo and an asphalt walkway—all which provide a haven of relaxation for employees during breaks.

In 1998, Reiman Publications was sold to Madison Dearborn Partners, a Chicago investment firm, and in 2002, it was resold to the Reader's Digest corporation.

Fortunately for Greendalers—many of whom are employed there—the company's publishing operations have not been moved, and the employee workforce has remained largely unchanged.

ARBOR and an abundance of flowers provide pleasing entrance to corporate offices of Reiman Publications.

CORPORATE PARK developed on the 29 acres by Reiman Publications provides long walking paths for employees.

PRETTY PLACE. View below looks down at rose gardens, gazebo, pond and fountain on Reiman Publications' grounds.

CHAPTER 39

Earlier Controversy Over Village Center

LET'S step back in time a bit: By 1958, the hub of stores on the west side of Broad Street became inadequate to serve the needs of the growing population. And so, on November 19, 1958, the area on the east side of the street gave way to bricks and mortar.

Soon gone were the giant elm tree, the bandstand and picnic areas that had served as the original gathering place and recreational haven for families for nearly 20 years. In their stead were 14 new stores, all connected as one long continuous struc-

ture. The project was undertaken by August Urbanek, the developer of the original store buildings.

Initial businesses opening on

EAST SIDE of Broad Street changed in 1958 when a long row of connected stores was built there.

the east side of the street included Al Dobner's Beer and Liquor Store, "Abe" Vielie's Rexall Drugstore, Seaman's Paint Store, Krambo's Food Store, Estelle's Sausage Shop, Casey's Greendale Grill and Bomberg's Bakery.

Hot butter-crust rolls were the top seller at the bakery, which became a popular spot on Sunday mornings.

"Everyone stopped there after church to buy hot ham and rolls," says Evelyn Truppe. "Those hot butter rolls were oh, so good! It was funny...you could tell what church service people were at because they came right from there to the bakery."

A major plan to modernize and enlarge the main street shopping center surfaced in 1959. The plan called for closing Broad Street on both ends and turning the area into a pedestrian mall, complete with additional shops and parking areas for some 600 to 800 cars. The advocates said this would greatly enlarge the village's tax base.

A private consulting firm was hired to design the project, but it quickly became mired in controversy over parking, traffic patterns and safety, along with the appropriation of land and relocation of existing buildings both east and west.

One plan called for moving Broad Street a good distance to the west, cutting through both Elementary School land and property occupied by St. Luke's Church.

Reroute Dale Creek?

A revised plan proposed that Broad Street be rerouted behind the shops on the east side. But that would require moving Dale Creek farther to the east.

Attached to this second concept was the plan to move Parking Street to the west at some point in the future. That, however, would necessitate demolishing the police and fire station and the public works building, and possibly the filling station at the corner of Parking Street and Northway, too.

According to the consulting firm's analysis, "The public works building is hopelessly inadequate, and the fire and police station will be

WEST SIDE of Broad Street started losing business tenants shortly after Southridge Shopping Center was developed north of Grange Avenue in 1970.

outgrown and useless soon anyway."

Yet another variation called for an overpass stretching from a two-story pavilion on the west side of Broad Street to professional offices on the east side.

After multiple meetings and sidewalk discussions, growing opposition by residents against any change affecting Broad Street finally convinced the Village Board to shelve the whole idea.

Typical of the public sentiment was expressed by Dale Neeb, of Elstead Avenue, who commented, "Our present village shopping facilities are nearly adequate. We may need a few more stores, but nothing as drastic as these planners propose. We don't want the beauty of our village destroyed for stores we don't need. Most of us came here because of the small-town atmosphere."

Even Elbert Peets was pulled into the controversy. In a letter opposing the proposed changes, the man who planned the village wrote, "Broad Street and Northway form the core of all Greendale. They set the tone of openness, good order, dignity and charm.

"Hundreds of people have come to live in Greendale as the result of a first impression formed as they drove through those two beautiful streets," he added. "Why change that now?"

As a result, any plans for a grand change came to naught. Broad Street still remains today as the single thoroughfare envisioned by its original planners.

Meanwhile, after the east side expansion was completed, Urbanek turned his attention to renovating and expanding the older buildings on the street's west side, from the tavern on the north end to the theatre building on the south end. Three new stores were added and six of the existing buildings were remodeled.

The redevelopment changed the appearance of these buildings to the same Colonial-Williamsburg style as the new stores on the east side, putting them in harmony with the styling of the Village Hall.

While the revitalized shopping center did well at first, the surge in retail traffic and sales didn't last. First, growing competition during the intervening years came from a commercial building boom that changed South 76th Street from a

> ## *"One early plan was to turn Broad Street into a pedestrian mall..."*

rural two-lane road into a mecca of commercial expansion.

The street was soon lined with small stores, office buildings and restaurants on both sides of the street from Grange Avenue all the way north to Layton Avenue, a stretch of about a mile. The changeover lured shoppers from Greendale to the new venues.

Then the nearly fatal ax for Greendale's village center fell in 1970, when Southridge Shopping Center

was developed along the east side of 76th Street. Farmland from Grange Avenue to Edgerton Avenue was graded and construction began on store after store.

The result was one of the largest malls in the nation at the time (and still the largest in Wisconsin at this writing). The first-class shopping center covered some 120 acres and included more than 130 stores and five major department stores.

On the positive side for Greendale, the huge mall generated property tax revenues that contributed nearly a quarter of the total taxes collected by the village in that era. It also provided employment opportunities for hundreds of residents.

On the negative side, customer traffic dropped off drastically in Greendale's village center as soon as the mall opened. And it steadily got worse. One by one, Broad Street shops began closing.

In retrospect, it was a classic case

CUSTOMER TRAFFIC declined sharply after Southridge opened. Shops soon began closing all along Broad Street.

OHIO INVESTORS never visited downtown Greendale in their last 12 years of ownership. With only seven of the 29 Broad Street businesses still open, the village center showed serious signs of decay. These photos were taken just prior to renovation that began in 1997.

of absentee ownership. The entire east side section of businesses was owned by an Ohio corporation.

It was pretty much a "paper investment"; locals contended that not one representative of the Ohio company had paid a single visit to Greendale in 12 years.

This lack of interest, unfortunately, was matched to some degree by the "give up" attitude of most of the Greendale shop owners.

Perhaps they could have mounted some sort of promotional campaign that told Milwaukeeans and people in the northern suburbs, "Now that you have a good reason to come to the south side, why not visit the charming, historic village of Greendale?" Instead, many just shook their head and gave up.

Became a "Ghost Town"

Predictably, the Ohio investors were unwilling to put any money into maintenance and cosmetic touches, because they didn't know how long the buildings would continue to be occupied.

The tenants, likewise, were unwilling to put up any of their own money into fix-ups because they didn't know how long they'd last.

By the early 1990s, only seven of the 29 Broad Street rental spaces were still open. And three of those were dental offices, which didn't really need main-street locations but had chosen to locate there because the rent had been lowered to attract any kind of business.

Gradually, the village center became somewhat of a ghost town. Many buildings were badly in need of paint, pieces of the facades and trim along the rooflines were broken, shingles were missing and windows were broken.

Many Greendalers bemoaned the appearance of their once-prosperous, attractive Greenbelt Town, but no one had a cure for it. A Greendale Promotions Committee was formed by Kathy Arciszewski in an attempt to attract new businesses to the area; however, the committee had little success.

To the chagrin of many who loved this little village, it appeared once-proud Greendale was doomed.

CHAPTER 40

The Rebirth of Greendale

THE REVIVED SPIRIT and face-lift that Broad Street sorely needed suddenly materialized in the fall of 1996. Local magazine publisher Roy Reiman announced that his Grandhaven investment firm would buy all the commercial properties along both sides of the village's main street!

The announcement promised an extensive renovation, with the aim of lifting the spirit of Greendale residents, while attracting commercial tenants who would offer specialized products and services not available at Southridge Shopping Center.

"My wife and I were just as saddened as other Greendale residents to watch what was slowly happening to this historic little town," Reiman relates. "We'd lived here for more than 30 years,

NEW Reiman Publications Visitor Center with carillon tower became attractive "anchor" on corner.

our kids had been well-served by the Greendale school system, and many of our 500-plus employees were from the Greendale area.

"The whole idea and concept of renovating the downtown area came to me one Saturday afternoon as I was walking through the woods near our house. I was mulling over the problem we were having at our corporate offices—too many of our subscribers were just 'stopping in for a visit' unannounced.

"It suddenly struck me that I could solve two problems at once if we could switch that traffic from our door to downtown Greendale. The merchants there needed the traffic; we needed to get rid of it."

Reiman explains the latter this way: "Our average subscriber is 57 years old. That means most of them are retired, and they love to travel. Since we publish these 'friendly' magazines, it seemed whenever any of these subscribers got close to Greendale, they'd just stop in at our offices for a visit.

"This was flattering on one hand, but frustrating on the other. They were all very nice people, but they kept showing up at our door, dozens of them. And they all wanted a tour.

"We didn't have a 'tour guide', so some busy editor (they always wanted to meet one of the editors) would be called to the reception area to meet them and walk them slowly through our offices.

"We'd finish touring a group of four, and soon there'd be another

---

"Greendale needed customer traffic, and we needed to get rid of it..."

---

group waiting at the door. Understandably, they were in no hurry whatsoever; but just as understandably, we had deadlines to meet.

"They wanted to walk through our facility, meet as many of our staff members as possible, then sit

down and visit. And if they ever got into our test kitchens, they didn't want to leave, period!

"Again, with narrow hallways and open cubicles, our facilities were never set up for tours. We're set up for publishing. Plus, the loud voices and laughter became a major distraction to creativity."

Finally, the company set a new policy: No more tours.

While Reiman agreed with the decision, he worried about the company's image and the disappointment of subscribers who came to the front door, eager to meet editors they'd come to know in print, and to see how and where the magazines and cookbooks were created.

"I was concerned about what they thought of us and what they told their friends," Reiman says. "I was afraid they went home and told 20 people, 'Sure, they put out those friendly magazines, but when you

CARILLON TOWER takes shape on corner of Reiman Visitor Center.

get to their front door, they tell you to go away!'"

So, that Saturday afternoon while walking in the woods, Reiman suddenly came up with the solution: Why not rent the old Dobner Liquor store on the corner downtown and turn it into a "company visitor center"? he mused.

"It could emulate all the things subscribers would normally see at the company—a working test kitchen, an editor's office, a display of items sent in by readers, a small theater with a video detailing the company's history, a 'bargain basement' offering closeout items from our catalog, etc., etc.

"We'd then *urge* our 15 million subscribers to 'Come for a visit' …but not to our offices. Instead, we'd invite them to this new Visitor Center in downtown Greendale.

"Perfect! That would steer subscribers away from our door and toward the village, where they were desperately needed."

Oops! Wait a Minute…

The more he thought about the idea, the more sense it made. But by the end of the weekend, a discouraging concern came to mind.

"I began to think about those Ohio investors, who hadn't done anything for this village in over 12 years," says Reiman.

"With this Visitor Center, customer traffic would gradually come back to the downtown area, and those investors would begin eagerly renting out all those closed business spaces. But…to whom?

"I just knew our subscribers would have a certain perception of what Greendale should be." (Reiman proved to be right about that. A friend of his was sitting on the bench in front of the Visitor Center, next to an older man wearing a "Michigan" cap. "Whaddaya think of Greendale?" the friend asked. Answered the fellow from Michigan: "It's exactly like I pictured it.")

So, Reiman reasoned, if the Ohioans continued to own the property, neither he nor Reiman Publications would have any control over

FLOOR-TO-CEILING windows of Reiman Visitor Center at installation stage.

the tenants. "They could have rented those empty spaces to adult bookstores, palm readers, tattoo parlors or whatever," he explains.

"Those things just wouldn't have 'fit' the image of the quaint, historic village we'd been describing to our subscribers for years before it started going downhill."

The only solution: Buy the buildings on both sides of Broad Street.

That would give him (and his company) total control over the selection of tenants. What's more, it would present the opportunity to give the village center a cosmetic makeover—with new storefronts, new lampposts, new trees and lots of flowers. Lots and lots of flowers. Reiman loves flowers.

Local Realtor Did the Deal

He knew, though, if his name or the company name was tied to the purchase, it would likely drive up the price. There would be the "regular price and the Reiman price", as he puts it.

So he contacted a well-regarded real estate developer, John O'Malley, who had grown up in the Greendale area, and had O'Malley confidentially represent him in the acquisition. The sellers likely assumed O'Malley had some new develop-

ment in mind and were eager to sell once approached.

"John did a great job for us," Reiman says. "And to show you the kind of guy he is, when we completed the transaction and I asked him what his fee was, John said, 'I grew up here, and that's my contribution to bringing this village back to life.' He wouldn't take a penny over his basic costs."

Reiman bought the properties through his family investment company, Grandhaven. His son, Scott, who heads up the company, took his father aside and said, "Dad, I hope you aren't looking at this as a good investment. This won't pay off in your lifetime or mine."

"I know," Reiman responded. "But some 'investments' are done for different reasons. I agree this will never pay off financially, but it can pay off in other ways—in a whole new spirit and enjoyment for this community's 15,000 residents, and the enjoyment of thousands of visitors, too.

"What's more, it can become a legacy to our company, its employees and our Greendale roots."

LARGE LOUNGE at Reiman Visitor Center allows subscribers from all parts of country a chance to get acquainted. An extensive Norman Rockwell display is now in part of this space.

TEST KITCHEN at the Visitor Center allows subscribers to see how recipes are tested for magazines and books. The company prepares and tests over 6,000 recipes a year!

CHAPTER 41

Village Gets New Face, New Future

WITH THE PURCHASE completed, the renovation began. The Milwaukee architectural firm of Uihlein-Wilson, which specializes in historic preservation projects, was chosen to design and handle the project.

To help the Village Board envision what the finished product would look like, a three-dimensional scale cardboard model (shown below) was constructed of the entire village center.

It showed the storefronts and new "boulevards" along Broad Street, new trees, green strips of grass and abundant flower beds.

After the firm won approval from the board for the go-ahead, the detailed model was displayed

MINIATURE MODEL below was used to help Village Board and residents "picture" the finished renovation.

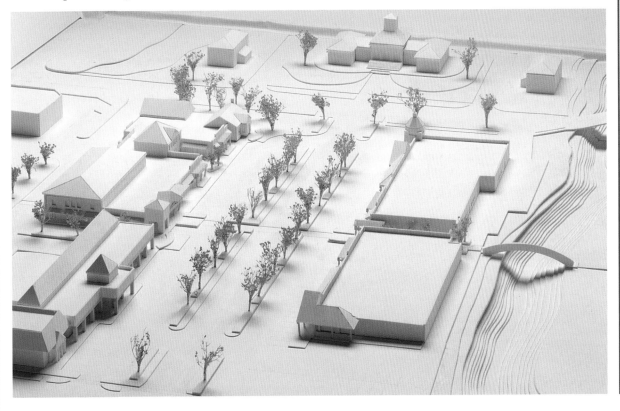

GREAT CARE was used to match village's original bricks. Even existing buildings were covered with "half bricks" (left). A tower was added on west side to "balance" new one on east side.

in a storefront along Broad Street, so residents could see and understand the end result.

Representatives of Uihlein-Wilson also made presentations at local group meetings, including the Chamber of Commerce, Lions Club and American Legion.

The architects emphasized their goal—to retain as much as possible of the village's 1930s nostalgic charm while "putting the green back in Greendale". They aimed to put more grass and flower beds amid the parking areas along Broad Street, while reconnecting the village center to Dale Park.

The latter was achieved by removing two business spaces along the east side of Broad Street to form a "corridor" there, then constructing an attractive walking bridge across Dale Creek (see next page).

When it was finished, this corridor and bridge had the desired effect—it once again gave residents direct access to the park. It allowed them to enjoy the spacious green area just as early Greendalers had before the span of buildings along the east side of the street blocked off the park.

Before the new corridor was completed, some residents didn't even know the park existed!

The ornate latticework of the white wooden arbor over the corridor has since proved so attractive it's become a favorite spot for wedding photos.

Great effort was taken by the designers to vary the roof height of the storefronts, especially those on the east side of Broad Street.

Those structures had all been one continuous flat-topped span of connected buildings. The renovation changed that dramatically. The fronts of those structures were varied 10 to 15 feet in height, with a tall "anchor" structure at both ends.

On the north end, this taller building was topped off with a small tower that houses a carillon; its bells mark each quarter hour and toll out patriotic songs several times a day.

A similar effort was made on the west side of the street, with a small tower atop the last structure on the south end. The effect is a matching anchor there.

The designers also took great care to retain the "New England feel" of the existing buildings. To do

FINISHED TOWER on west side and varied height of storefronts added eye appeal. New nostalgic lampposts each hold two large flower baskets.

BEFORE AND AFTER. Two business spaces were removed (above) to make room for a "corridor" to reconnect the village center with Dale Park. Below is the finished effect, with new bridge over Dale Creek at right. It's become a favorite wedding photo site.

ELEANOR'S FOUNTAIN honors Eleanor Roosevelt. Plaques along its base tell of her visit and village's history.

so, more than a dozen different types and colors of bricks were tested and compared before choosing one to match the original bricks used in the '30s. The match was close—it's now difficult to detect where the old and the new are blended.

The renovation was extensive, down to the last detail. Damaged windows were replaced, door and window trim was repaired and repainted, and a whole new roof was added to the old post office building.

A large fountain was constructed in front of the old post office. It's called "Eleanor's Fountain", in honor of Eleanor Roosevelt's visit to the village. Large metal plaques surrounding the fountain tell the gist of Greendale's history in chronological order.

New trees were planted all along Broad Street, and nostalgic lampposts were added. The golden hue of these lights gives the street a glow reminiscent of gaslight days.

The arms of each lamppost hold two large flower baskets that provide a plethora of blooms throughout the summer and fall seasons.

"My wife and I got the idea for these lampposts during a trip to Victoria on Vancouver Island," explains Reiman. "They must have a hundred of them, each holding huge double baskets filled with flowers. 'That's what we want for Greendale!' I said and took a picture to show our architect."

There's a funny follow-up to that: Several years later, a man came up to Reiman at a wedding reception and asked, "Have you ever been to Victoria in Canada? They swiped your idea for those light poles and flower baskets!"

"No," Reiman corrected him, "sorry—we copied theirs."

Lighthearted moments like that were the upside of the renovation. But there were more than a few unexpected downsides.

First, there was the large amount of asbestos in the buildings. The cost of removing it from the old theatre alone ran over $75,000.

Smelly Problem Surfaces

But nothing was worse than what Grandhaven was confronted with when digging began next to the old tavern to prepare a basement for the new restaurant planned there. All of a sudden there was a strong, strange odor, and heavy contamination was expected.

The DNR was called in, and construction was stopped immediately. The resulting study determined that a dry goods cleaner formerly located next to the tavern had, for years, simply run their chemicals out a pipe and onto the ground. Digging showed the soil was badly contaminated as much as 25 feet down!

At this point, DNR officials gave Grandhaven two choices: Either leave the remaining building an empty shell, with no occupancy allowed. Or totally remove the soil.

"We really didn't have a choice," Reiman recalls. "We'd gone this far with the renovation—we couldn't

NEW BRIDGE (top) is set in place over Dale Creek. At right is interior of Reiman Visitor Center during construction.

"FLOWER BED BOULEVARDS" were built along both sides of Broad Street.

BIG STINK. And the cost was even worse when serious contamination was found while digging along Broad Street. DNR officials stopped construction, and Grandhaven had no choice but to haul the bulk of the contaminated soil to a site in Indiana and the worst of it to a site in Canada. Below are some of the trucks lining up for the long hauls. The cleanup took over 6 months to complete.

just leave this empty eyesore at one end. After all, this was the 'entrance' at Broad Street where most people come into the village."

It was even worse than first thought: The soil was so contaminated that no Wisconsin site would accept it! The bulk of it was eventually hauled to one site in Indiana, and some of it had to be hauled as far as Canada.

The digging and removal was extensive. Semi trucks lined up along Broad Street (see picture at left) to handle the task.

The contamination cleanup took more than 6 months, delaying completion of the renovation project. Grandhaven officials declined to give the total cost of the cleanup. But one of them admitted it was so extreme, the cost ended up matching the total construction costs of the new restaurant.

New Tenants See Potential

The total renovation of the village center took more than 2 years to complete. Even before it was finished, small business owners from other areas began showing interest, and leases were signed.

"We were very selective in the

types of tenants we chose," says Anne Marie Pelkofer, Grandhaven's village center manager. "We had two goals—we wanted to choose businesses that benefited Greendale residents first and visitors second. And we didn't want to duplicate anything Southridge Shopping Center already offered."

Another goal was to choose tenants who not only sold something but also taught something in order to benefit the community. As a result,

ROOF ADDED. When the renovation architect looked at the old post office (right), he said, "The original builders either ran out of time or money—with windows that close to the top, they were definitely planning a roof for that structure." So one was added (below), which greatly improved building's appearance.

GOOD RIDDANCE TO FLAT TOPS. The singular line of continuous buildings on the east side of Broad Street built in 1958 (above) had one level roofline. In the renovation (below), the front roofline was attractively varied (as shown along west side in photo at right). The two businesses in the center of photo above were removed to make way for the "corridor" to Dale Park.

PRETTY VIEW of west side of Broad Street after renovation was completed.

Broad Street businesses now offer classes in crafting, stained glass window design, woodworking and more. Such classes have become so popular that when Glassic Designs opened, for example, the shop's classes were sold out months in advance.

Prior to the renovation, a number of village center tenants were trying to get out of their leases and relocate at Southridge. Since the Broad Street renovation, several Southridge tenants have been trying to move to Greendale!

One couple who succeeded is Dick and Sylvia Maslowski, who operate Heavenly Presence. They had run their business at Southridge for over 20 years before relocating to the village center.

"We're doing much more business here," says Dick. "Plus, I like the fact that here I can step outside to see the sun and flowers and chat with visitors. We love it here!"

All 27 of the business spaces in the village center are now fully rented, with inquiries coming in from other tenants eager to locate there.

"We're very pleased with the variety of businesses we have," says Pelkofer. "We have a good choice of restaurants and food services to serve the locals, plus a selection of

> ### *"Even before the renovation was finished, new tenants began showing interest..."*

unique gift and craft shops to serve visitors and residents as well."

An estimated 200,000 people now visit Greendale annually. Little wonder, since the 15 million-plus subscribers to Reiman Publications' 13 national magazines are often encouraged to "Come for a visit!"

These magazines reach a huge audience. With more than 3.2 readers per copy, over 50 million people read the publications. It's estimated that one in every 12 homes

in America now receives at least one Reiman magazine.

Subscribers are urged to visit through periodic articles detailing the village's unique "Greenbelt Town" history and illustrated with beautiful photos. As a result, many visitors appear to know a good deal about the village before they arrive.

Again and again—especially at Christmastime, when all the buildings on both sides of Broad Street are outlined in over 100,000 holiday lights—visitors say, "This place looks just like a Norman Rockwell greeting card!"

That comment was heard so often, Reiman bought an entire Rockwell collection—including every one of the 322 covers Rockwell painted for *The Saturday Evening Post*—and moved it to Greendale. That exhibit, now on display in the downtown area, helps the village appear even more like a "Rockwell Town".

FLOWERS EVERYWHERE. Over 37,000 flowers are planted downtown each spring. Above are the new nostalgic lampposts, which glow reminiscent of gaslight days, each supporting two large flower baskets. Below is archway entrance to Dale Park.

CHAPTER 42

New Ideas Keep Greendale Exciting

SHORTLY AFTER the renovation was complete, Grandhaven management formed a Greendale Business Association, with each new tenant becoming a member and thereby having a voice.

Each tenant was asked to contribute toward a promotion budget, then Grandhaven matched the total of those funds. This group

meets regularly to suggest promotional programs and also to discuss problems and opportunities. They're even asked their opinion of prospective new tenants before the lease is signed.

The Business Association has come up with a number of successful events, some of which have become annual affairs. One

of these popular events is "Dickens of a Christmas", which is held on the first Friday night of De-

PRISTINE VIEW of the Village Hall below personifies the "Rockwell Town" label. Greendale's designer, Elbert Peets, was fond of the main building at Williamsburg in Virginia, so he made the Village Hall a miniature copy of it—right to the rooster on its tower.

"IT LOOKS LIKE A 'NORMAN ROCKWELL' TOWN!" That's heard from visitors often, particularly during the holiday season, when all the Broad Street buildings are outlined with over 100,000 twinkling lights, and Christmas carols are played from the carillon tower. Note the large Santa climbing the wall of Ricardo's restaurant in the photo below.

cember. The shopkeepers dress in Victorian costumes for the evening, and each year more of those who attend come in costume as well.

Carriage rides are offered...carolers sing along Broad Street... chestnuts are roasted...kettle corn adds a sweet aroma...and local schoolteachers reenact a portion of "The Ghosts of Christmas Past".

This event is attended by thousands of people eager to get into the holiday spirit. When soft snow falls on this evening, Greendale truly personifies a "Rockwell town".

Events Draw Thousands

Another popular annual event is "Hay Days" each autumn, featuring pumpkin carving and scarecrow contests. Equally popular is the "Emerald Event", featuring characters from *The Wizard of Oz* (at right).

Another spring event that drew well was an "I Left My Heart on Broad Street" affair with a Tony Bennett look-alike contest.

And parades? It seems Greendalers hardly need a reason to stage another colorful parade down Broad Street. There's a Memorial Day parade, school homecoming parades and a Fourth of July parade.

The latter draws thousands of viewers, lasts nearly 2 hours and exudes a "small town" image with children's festively decorated bikes, coaster wagons and scooters among multiple bands and local performers.

There's also a parade during Village Days held in August. Hundreds of early residents and their children return to celebrate the anniversary of Greendale's beginning, walk through craft booths in Dale Park, listen to the village concert band or just sit in one of the tents and enjoy corn on the cob, hamburgers, hot dogs and ice cream sundaes while catching up with old friends.

Always Something Happening

A great effort goes into keeping a good deal of "fun" in Greendale all year long. Free outdoor concerts are held every Saturday and Sunday night during summer in the large gazebo on Broad Street.

Hundreds of residents bring lawn

chairs and blankets for these weekend musical events. One night when an orchestra played "The Big Band Sound", local police got into the spirit of the occasion and temporarily blocked off Broad Street so residents could dance in the street. And did they ever!

This large eight-sided gazebo, which has gradually become Greendale's new "gathering place", has an interesting history of its own.

Back in the early '90s, one longtime resident, Bob Drews, lamented the loss of the green space on the east side of Broad Street. He remembered the good times he'd

FUN-FILLED WEEKENDS in Greendale include the "Emerald Event", with several original *Wizard of Oz* characters in attendance. Locals get in the spirit by dressing in *Oz* costumes. Above are Brian Sienko as the "Tin Man" and Katie Rose Pelkofer as "Dorothy".

enjoyed there as a youth, before 14 new stores were built in that space.

It was where the pioneers gathered under the giant elm tree on Sunday afternoons for picnics and for evening concerts at the bandstand. It was where village children played softball and other games on warm summer days.

Drews' vision was to re-create

that venue in the open space just south of Schoolway on the east side of Broad Street. He led efforts to acquire 1 acre of land there for a $1-a-year lease from Milwaukee County, which owns it as part of the Root River system.

Following approval by the Village Board, Drews moved on—he contacted local volunteer organizations, asking each to designate a representative to serve on a committee which would screen ideas for the design of a gazebo at the site.

Unique Fund-Raising Idea

The committee held its first meeting on August 28, 1994. In addition to Drews, the committee was made up of James Clinton, Pat Koth, Sally Chadwick, Warren Atkinson, Marie Birmingham, Barbara Brunett, Joan Dembosky, John Munger, Bette Murray, William Poglitsch, Elaine Rendleman, Marji Singer and Vera Westman. Also included were two gazebo designers, Ed Halbeck and Sharon Pendleton.

Funds for the project were raised by the committee in a novel fashion. Anyone who contributed $25 or more could have their family name or other wording engraved in a brick that would form the gazebo floor. A total of 1,584 of these "memorialized" bricks were funded.

With financing in hand, volunteers—spearheaded by the local Lions Club—began constructing the gazebo on May 8, 1995. It quickly became a community project that energized individuals and businesses to donate their services.

Bernie Schroedl, who served as village president from 1984 to 1988, used his Wenta Monument Company's equipment to engrave all the bricks—free.

Jack and Jim Reichl, two brothers, grew up in Greendale, had their company, Reichl Construction, install all the bricks for free—*twice*! When the first installation "just did not look right" to them, they had workers pull up the bricks and laid them all a second time—at no charge.

The wrought-iron hangers were designed by Bob Haase, and the rooster weather vane atop the cupola was a gift paid for with funds raised by the Greendale Village Quilters. The hanging baskets are donated yearly by Grandhaven.

The finished gazebo was dedicated on August 13, 1995, during that year's Village Days celebration. The ceremony included a concert by the Greendale Community Band, conducted by John Munger.

The New "Gathering Place"

That became the first of many concerts there. The gazebo also soon became a popular locale for wed-

ALL DECKED OUT for Fourth of July weekend, the gazebo's ready for the band.

FREE CONCERTS make the gazebo a popular spot on summer weekends. Hundreds of locals and visitors bring lawn chairs, blankets and coolers.

dings, graduation pictures and other family events. The first couple to say their marriage vows under its welcoming roof were Jonathan Strand and Tracy de Priest on October 14, 1995.

Now known as Greendale Gazebo Park, it's the site of free concerts on Saturday and Sunday evenings all summer long. Booking of the Saturday performers is han-

> ## *"Ernie Borgnine loved the local concerts…"*

dled by the Greendale Entertainment Committee, and the Sunday concerts are scheduled by the Greendale Park & Recreation Association. A community umbrella organization, the Greendale Public Celebrations Committee, oversees these and other village events.

Weekend evenings at the park are something to behold, with hundreds of residents (over 800 people were counted one evening) carrying lawn chairs and blankets to favorite spots as the sun drops low. The acoustics of the gazebo send the concert music far beyond the village center.

One Saturday evening, Academy Award winner Ernie Borgnine—who was in Milwaukee to participate in the city's annual Circus Parade—was brought to the concert by Greendale friends.

He looked over the smiling crowd, soaked up the atmosphere and said, "People in Beverly Hills should see this. This is small-town entertainment at its best. This is a slice of Americana!"

A TEENAGE GROUP, called "Accompany of Kids", performs at one of the Saturday concerts. Below, the gazebo's dressed up for winter—it's decorated annually by volunteers to fit in with other holiday decor that enhances village's "Rockwell Town" image.

CHAPTER 43

Now 'Jewel' of Milwaukee Suburbs

AFTER the renovation of the downtown was completed in 1998, there was a small period of adjustment for Greendalers. While new business tenants appreciated the immediate increase in customer traffic, residents seemed a little surprised by it.

Just 2 years prior, there were so few cars in the downtown area that tenants tended to park in front of their own stores; now they and others had to look for a parking place. Some residents even complained that they had to walk "all the way across the street" to a particular business.

Police Chief Rob Dams put this in perspective when he said, "This village has needed a parking problem for a long time. This place was dying, now it's alive again. Most residents will gladly trade a longer walk for the new energy and lively pace this village now has."

This "energy" is still obvious on any day of the week. Thousands of visitors—many of them subscribers drawn to the "headquarters town" of Reiman Publications—have come to regard Greendale as a travel destination.

A large percentage of these friendly folks are retired (the average age of Reiman subscribers is 57). So most of them are not in the kind of hurry that's associated with the frantic pace of large shopping malls.

They take time to appreciate and photograph the flower beds along Broad Street...they read the plaques at Eleanor's Fountain to

---

"The flowers are cared for by volunteers called 'Weed-Out Warriors'..."

---

learn a bit of Greendale's history...they walk a few blocks to take a closer look at the village's famed "backward houses"...they browse the stores and chat with business owners...some even buy sandwiches from the deli or ice cream shop to enjoy a picnic lunch in Dale Park.

Adds Interest for Locals

Greendale residents who take time to do so enjoy visiting with these out-of-towners. A large map in the Reiman Visitor Center—

which encourages people to "Pinpoint where you're from" by sticking a pin in their hometown —provides evidence that visitors not only come from every state, but from all over the world.

One business owner says this is what makes each day incredibly interesting. "Every day it's like taking a 'trip' of my own," he relates. I meet people from everywhere and learn what life is like where they live. Yesterday I visited with someone from New Orleans in the morning and someone from a small town in Switzerland in the afternoon."

Likely no one enjoys these visitor-conversations more than Greendale's own retirees, many of whom gather daily at "The Birdhouse Workshop". The space for this cheerful facility was provided rent-free by Grandhaven, the firm that revitalized the village's downtown area.

The firm also contributed all of the facility's tools, lumber, shelving and other necessary equipment as a way of "giving something back to local seniors". The shop, located right next to the Reiman Publications Visitor Cen-

187

HAPPY HELPERS at Birdhouse Workshop turn out colorful miniature replicas of "Greendale originals".

BIRDHOUSE FOR SALE...cheep.

ter, gives these retirees an opportunity to gather with friends and create woodcrafted items, primarily birdhouses, most of which are miniature replicas of "Greendale originals" (see above).

The "job description" posted on the front door during its first year set the tone for this lighthearted group. "Excellent benefits. Totally flexible hours. Come and go as you please. No boss, no pressure, no dress code, no deadlines, no production schedules, no sales quotas, no nothing," the large poster stated.

Then it added: "There's only one

catch: There's no salary, either."

Yet the "pay" and the "benefits" are substantial for those "working" there. The shop gives local seniors a place to go, something to do and new visitors to talk to each day, making their time there all the more enjoyable.

These energetic "elves" sell their creations—which now include a wide variety of woodcrafted items —to visitors and residents.

Part of the revenue is used to help finance community events (such as the weekend gazebo concerts), and part of it goes into a "pool" that covers the group's costs of trips to theatrical performances, historical sites and the like, plus pizza parties and other functions.

The "guys" at the shop do most of the building, and the "gals" do most of the painting. The impressive results are often regarded as "works of art". Many customers say the birdhouses are "way too pretty to hang outdoors".

Nevertheless, many residents now have these houses in their yards, helping turn Greendale into a literal birds and blooms haven.

Speaking of blooms, flowers is the one thing any summer visitor is sure to notice in Greendale. And

with more than 37,000 annuals planted each spring in beds, baskets, pots and window boxes, it's no wonder. It's noteworthy that the care of all these flowers is undertaken in good part by more than 60 Greendale volunteers.

Flowers Everywhere

The idea came from Reiman, who explains, "There's a senior apartment facility within walking distance of the village center, and one of those residents mentioned how much she missed her flowers and garden since she sold her home and moved into her apartment.

"I gave it some thought, then simply swiped the concept of the 'Adopt a Highway' program and began an 'Adopt a Plot' program here. It was an immediate hit. Any resident can 'adopt' as large or small a plot along Broad Street as they'd like.

"We put a small sign in each bed, 'This Plot Cared for by Ella Smith' or whomever. Grandhaven takes care of the watering and fertilizing, but these volunteers take care of all the weeding and deadheading.

"They do a terrific job and enjoy

the sense of involvement. We give the volunteers a newly designed shirt each spring that says 'WOW' in large letters on the front. That stands for 'Weed-Out Warriors'. On the back of the shirt it says, 'We're making Greendale the best blooming town in the country!'

"It may be corny, but it works. What's really gratifying is to hear visitors say they're going to start a program just like this in their town when they get back home."

Greendale has also become known for its daffodils. That all started as a result of an article written in Reiman Publications' *Birds & Blooms* magazine. It announced plans to plant a large daffodil garden in Dale Park so it could be referred to as "Daffo*dale* Park".

This large flower garden would be designed in the shape of a "sun", with the sun planted in red tulips, and the daffodils planted in 50 long rows to form the "rays" spreading out from the sun.

Why 50 rays? There would be one row for each state—Alabama through Wyoming—and the bulbs from each state would be planted in their respective row. (Ultimately

---

"More than 54,000 daffodil bulbs were sent to Greendale!"

---

there were 51 rows, with an extra one added for bulbs received from Canadian subscribers.)

The aim was to make Greendale "The Daffodale Capital of the Country", the article stated. To get the project under way, Grandhaven would donate 2,000 bulbs for the daffodil garden. Subscribers were told they could consider sending in a few bulbs of their own, so one day they could say they helped make Greendale the "daffodale capital".

After the issue with this article

went in the mail, the editors and Grandhaven staff waited to see what kind of response it would receive. In 2 weeks, they were surprised. In 3 weeks, they were amazed. And in a month, they were overwhelmed.

More than *54,000 daffodil bulbs* were received from subscribers! Some contributors had sent two or three, but others sent a dozen or more, with notes saying how proud they were to have their bulbs be part of making Greendale known for its abundance of daffodils.

They'd all followed the recommended directions, too, cleaning soil off the freshly dug bulbs, inserting them in a plastic bag and attaching their name to the package.

On one hand, the editors were delighted; on the other hand, they were now facing a dilemma: Only 7,000

"WEED-OUT WARRIORS" are local volunteers who adopt individual flower beds along Broad Street and do all the weeding and deadheading.

DAFFODIL BED in Dale Park is one of a kind. More than *54,000 bulbs* were sent in for the garden by Reiman Publications subscribers! It was planted in the shape of a large "sun"—red tulips form the sun, and daffodils planted in 50 rows (one for each state) form the golden "rays". Bulbs from respective states are in each row, alphabetically from Alabama to Wyoming, and are identified with small signs at the end of each row. Some of these signs are apparent in the photo below.

bulbs were needed to plant the "sun bed". What would they do with the *47,000 extra bulbs*, now stored in a huge pile in the basement of the hardware store?

After giving it some thought, they came up with a solution. They announced in the local newspaper that, on a specified Saturday, Greendale residents could pick up as many of the bulbs as they wanted, as long as they showed their driver's license to assure they were locals. But each recipient had to promise two things:

1. That they would plant the bulbs in their front yard so the daffodils could be seen from the street and appreciated by people driving through the village.

2. That they would save the donor's name and address, then send a "thank you" note and a photo when the flowers were in full bloom.

As a result of the second provi-

TRANQUIL VIEW down Broad Street toward the village's signature building, the Village Hall, captures the full essence of today's renovated Greendale.

sion, "daffodil connections" were soon formed across the country. Many donors and recipients started corresponding, and in some cases they developed such a friendship that the two parties have even visited back and forth.

Springs Are Now Golden

Since daffodils propagate quickly, the number of yellow and gold blooms has annually doubled and redoubled throughout the village.

Plus, Grandhaven plants several thousand more additional bulbs each fall in selected areas, further enhancing the village's growing image as the "Daffodale Capital".

As for the original daffodil garden in Dale Park, the "rays" of the sun have multiplied and grown together, yielding a welcome burst of bloom each spring.

The garden isn't left idle after the daffodils die out in mid-May. Gold marigolds are then planted in the "sun", and red salvia is planted to replace the "rays", offering summer-long beauty for the park's frequent visitors.

By the end of May, the 37,000-plus annuals planted in Broad Street beds, hanging baskets and storefront pots are ready to add their brilliance to the village center. Complementing these blooms are 3,000 flowering trees that have been planted in the village since the renovation.

Adding a deep-red color to the hue is a bed of roses just across the bridge in Dale Park. Those roses were planted there for a special reason: That variety—the "Knockout Rose"—was named Rose of the Year by the National Rose Society in 2001. And that very rose was developed in the basement of a Greendale home in the 1970s.

A Robust Rebound

Perhaps the best way to recapture and appreciate the long and unique journey that has taken Greendale and its people to this time and day is to stand on the steps of the Village Hall and gaze down Broad Street.

The effect is best late on a quiet summer evening, as shadows are lengthening and the sun is softening the colors of the street's bountiful flowers, vibrant trees and green-grass expanses.

The sights and sounds combine both yesterday and today. The street still holds the hopes and dreams of those pioneers who persevered here …it's truly the symbol of their tribulations and triumphs. But it also echoes the spirit and vision of those who followed and enriched this historical village ever since.

From a town with a blighted village center that faced oblivion in 1996, Greendale—thanks to the joint efforts of Grandhaven, hundreds of volunteers and a Village Board that carefully plotted its future—has robustly rebounded.

Today it's often called "the jewel of Milwaukee's suburbs" by Wisconsinites who frequent its quaint shops and homey restaurants.

More importantly, its history and ambience have become so well known to a wider audience that the village has become a travel destination, attracting thousands of visitors from across the U.S. and abroad.

Greendale. It's truly the little village that could…and did.